The Real Musashi

The Real Musashi

Also by William de Lange

Iaido

Pars Japonica

A Dictionary of Japanese Idioms

Famous Japanese Swordsmen, three volumes

The Real Musashi, Origins of a Legend I: The *Bushū Denraiki*

THE REAL MUSASHI

Origins of a Legend II

The *Bukōden*

TRANSLATED AND ANNOTATED BY WILLIAM DE LANGE

FLOATING WORLD EDITIONS

First edition, 2011

Published by Floating World Editions, Inc.
26 Jack Corner Road, Warren, CT 06777
www.floatingworldeditions.com

Printed in the U.S.A.

ISBN 978-1-891640-60-5

Library of Congress Cataloging-in-Publication data available

For Kyōko Endō

Table of Contents

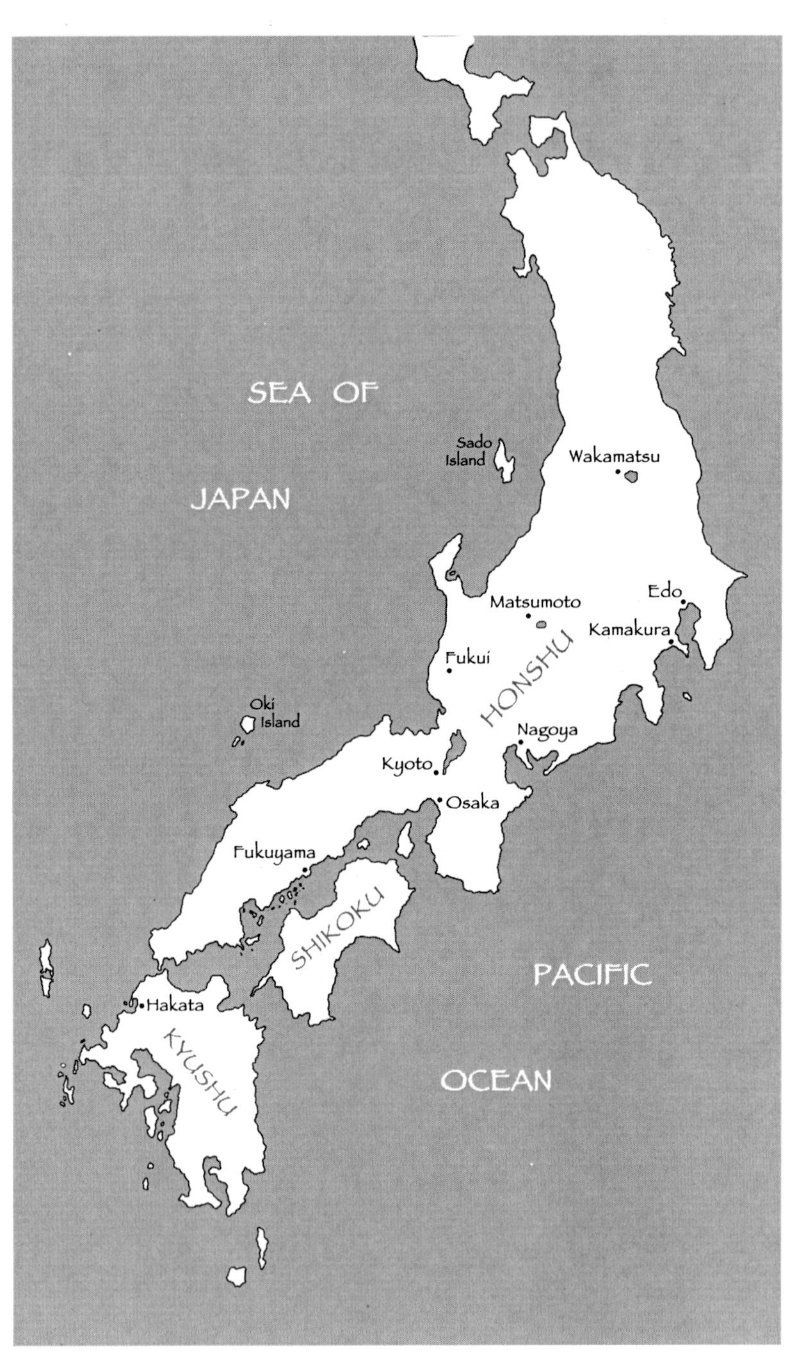

SEA OF
JAPAN
PACIFIC
OCEAN
HONSHU
SHIKOKU
KYUSHU
Sado Island
Wakamatsu
Matsumoto
Edo
Kamakura
Fukui
Oki Island
Nagoya
Kyoto
Osaka
Fukuyama
Hakata

Introduction

The Legend of Miyamoto Musashi

No swordsman in Japanese history is so revered and celebrated as Miyamoto Musashi. In Japan alone close to a thousand works have taken Musashi as their subject, many in the form of novels, the first one appearing as far back as the turn of the eighteenth century. Even now, more than four and a half centuries after his last exploits, hardly a year passes by without the lone swordsman turning up in some newly released film or television adaptation.

Sadly, amid this veritable deluge of books, comics, films, television soaps, and docudramas, little room is given to the old *denki*, the early biographies that were written by men who, though they may not have known Musashi alive, faithfully recorded what had been passed down to them by men who had. This is especially the case since most of what is known about Musashi today is based on the vivid recollections of these very men. Indeed, together with the *Bushū denraiki* the *Bukōden* is considered among the most reliable records about Musashi's life outside, of course, the writings by the master swordsman himself. Thier value is increased by Musashi's own reticence about his exploits, to which, in his *Book of Five Rings*, he dedicates no more than a few paragraphs.

Given Musashi's huge popularity, many of the more human aspects of this medieval warrior have with time been relegated to the margins in favor of a highly polished portrayal of his undisputed fencing skills. The resulting image is one of an invincible war-machine, a two-dimensional and hollow caricature, bereft of the personal traits that make us all human.

It is all the more exciting, then, to return to these earliest of records to find behind the myth a man of real flesh, who in spite of his unparalleled mastery of the sword has all the traits and idiosyncrasies to which all of us are prone. We discover that he was an extraordinarily precocious youth who had a deeply troubled relationship with his father. That background, combined with his rather disheveled physical appearance, may well have been one of the driving forces behind his desire to impress his friends in youth and champion over his adversaries when he reached adulthood. We discover that in old age he was often short-tempered, had no time for fools, and could be merciless with anyone who crossed his path. At the same time we learn that he could also be caring, that he was protective of his pupils, and that he adopted two young men and helped them to good positions with those in power. Perhaps most surprisingly, we discover that he had an illegitimate child, a girl who tragically died in childhood — an experience that must have marked him for life.

The aim of this work is to return to one of these earliest of records in order to unravel some of the legend and thereby recapture the real character of this enigmatic medieval swordsman. In following this rarely trodden trail the reader will soon find that the newly gained insights into Musashi's personality do not in the least diminish his stature but only serve to make him a more rounded character, a human being with whom we can all identify.

❷ The Origins of the Legend

Among the early biographies of Miyamoto Musashi four works stand out in particular. They are the *Bushū denraiki*, the *Heihō senshi denki*, the *Bukōden*, and the *Nitenki*. All four works were written during the eighteenth century, and all four were written by renowned masters of Musashi's Niten Ichi school of swordsmanship. Yet while all four works equally concern themselves with Musashi's life and exploits they represent two separate narrative strands. To understand this distinction it is necessary to take a closer look at each work and its author.

The earliest and for that simple reason arguably most reliable work is the *Bushū denraiki* [previously translated by this author and published as *The Real Musashi, Origins of a Legend (I)*]. It was written in 1727 by Tanji Hōkin, alias Tachibana Minehide, an inhabitant of the province of Chikuzen and a former retainer of the house of Kuroda, a clan closely associated with Musashi's early military career. The *Heihō senshi denki* was written half a century later, in 1782. Its author was Hōkin's former pupil, who had lost his master's writings and sought to recapture for posterity what he remembered. The *Bukōden* was written in 1755 by Toyoda Masanaga. Masanaga hailed from the nearby province of Higo and was a senior retainer to the Nagaoka (Matsui), vassals of the Hosokawa clan, who were closely associated to events in Musashi's later life. The *Nitenki*, finally, was written in 1776 by Masanaga's son Kagehide. Given that he succeeded his father as fencing instructor to the Nagaoka and inherited his father's writings, Kagehide had no reason to recapture what he already possessed. His aim, rather, was to improve on his father's work and make it more accessible.

It is clear, then, that the *Bushū denraiki* and its spin-off, the *Heihō senshi denki*, represent one narrative tradition. They recount the events of Musashi's life as they were originally perceived and recorded by Tachibana Minehine. The *Bukōden* and its spin-off, the *Nitenki*, by contrast recount the events of Musashi's life as they were originally perceived and recorded by Toyoda Masanaga. It is true that both Minehine's star pupil and Masanaga's son brought their own particular insights and experiences to Musashi's art of fencing, but in essence their works are derivative and contribute little of great value to the works of their predecessors in historical terms.

Given that all works were written well after their subject had passed away it should not surprise us that many an anecdote of doubtful origin has insinuated its way into their lines since Musashi's death. As with all such works, all four records contain accounts of events that, when held up against the light of historical fact, simply cannot have taken place—at least not in the way described.

Nevertheless, apart from Musashi's *Book of Five Rings* (of which only copies survive today), these biographies are the chief source on which modern historians and authors alike have based their accounts. It is well known, for instance that the twentieth century novelist Yoshikawa Eiji drew heavily though freely on these existing records when, between 1935 and 1939, his hugely popular *Miyamoto Musashi* appeared in serialized form in the *Asahi shinbun*, totaling more than a thousand episodes. Though the most widely read, Eiji was not the only author inspired by Musashi's exploits. Hundreds of others have over time directed their energies toward the same subject, be it in fiction or the most astutely academic of works. But like Yoshikawa all of them have in some form or other drawn on those first brave attempts to capture on paper the man Musashi.

To blindly trust these works is fraught with considerable danger. The idea, for instance, that Musashi participated in the Battle of Sekigahara (1600) is largely due to the misreading of these four pivotal works. Such misreading may have been willful. To have Musashi fight on the part of the losing side (as happens in Yoshikawa's work), after all, provides far more scope for dramatic development. They have, however, no root in historical fact. Nor, for that matter, in any of the early biographies. Only the *Bukōden* seems to suggest that Musashi was anywhere near Sekigahara during the battle but in lines that are so few and so vague as to be without meaning. Those who carefully study all available records will soon find that Musashi could not have taken part in the battle, let alone on the side of the western forces. The *Bushū denraiki*, for one, is clear enough about the side on which Musashi found himself fighting in the epic confrontations that marked the closing days of the period of civil strife. In its opening lines it unequivocally states that both Musashi and his father served the Kuroda clan, one of Tokugawa Ieyasu's most loyal allies. It goes on to describe in great detail how—while the Battle of Sekigahara was being fought out near Lake Biwa—Musashi joined his lord, Kuroda Toshitaka, in battle on the southern island of Kyushu, a claim backed by recently uncovered records in the Kuroda estate. Another misconception is that during the siege of Osaka castle Musashi fought on the side of the castle's defenders. Though both the *Bushū denraiki* and the *Bukōden* fail to mention under whom Musashi served, recent research has proven beyond doubt that he again fought on the side of the eastern forces, this time under the command of Mizuno Katsunari, another close vassal of Ieyasu.

It is, however, rather in their many points of convergence than in their discrepancies that the four works—and in particular the *Bushū denraiki* and the *Bukōden*—give us cause for celebration. Whether it be his first duel with Arima Kihei, his bouts with the Yoshioka brothers, or his famous duel with Sasaki on Ganryū island, all of the major events in Musashi's life are recounted in remarkably similar detail. This consistency is quite astonishing when one considers the historical gap of half a century that lies between the conception of the two works—all the more so given the absence of any indications that Masanaga was in any way influenced by Hōkin's work when he wrote his *Bukōden*.

Despite their compatibility the two works nevertheless present us with two different perspectives of Musashi's life. The *Bukōden* represents Musashi's story as it was passed down by retainers of the Hosokawa clan. It is to be expected, then, that the *Bukōden* tends to emphasize those parts of Musashi's life and exploits that reflect well on the Hosokawa. As for instance, Hosokawa Tadatoshi's role in the gestation of the *Book of Five Rings*. Hōkin, by contrast, represents Musashi's story as it was passed down by retainers of the Kuroda. Not surprisingly, the *Bushū denraiki* stresses those incidents that reflect well on the Kuroda clan and tends to gloss over others, as for instance Musashi's choice in old age to move to Kumamoto instead of nearby Fukuoka, the fief ruled by the Kuroda, who were, after all, the clan under whom his father had served and under whom he himself had began his military career. The two oral traditions, in short, present two views of the man Musashi as it was passed down and spread among the ranks of two different clans, with different traditions and different perspectives on the role of the warrior in a by then largely peaceful society.

There is another marked difference in nuance between the two works, for while they both describe Musashi's life from his birth to his death they do not cover the details of that life in equal depth. This difference is simply due to the fact that Musashi spent much of his youth in the domain of the Kuroda clan, while he spent his last days in the domain of the Hosokawa clan. As a result, the *Bushū denraiki* is rich in details on Musashi's early life, while the *Bukōden* is far more knowledgeable on how Musashi spent the last years of his life. Thus, Hōkin, who had held high office among the retainers of the Kuroda clan, is able to reveal facets of Musashi's early life that cannot be found in the *Bukōden*, as, for instance, Musashi's participation in the sieges of Aki and Tomiku castle, at a time when he was sixteen years old. Conversely, Masanaga, who had long served the Hosakowa as chief retainer—and thus intimately at home with the history of all who had served them—was able to describe in great detail the way in which Musashi's spent his last days in the Reigan

Cave and the gestation of the *Book of Five Rings*, an episode that Hōkin had to glean from outside sources.

Far from contradicting each other and thereby diminishing each other's value, the two works tend to complement each other in two important ways. One, by providing their own specific details on those episodes they have in common. More importantly, both works recount their own unique anecdotes. Musashi's bout with the Yagyū Shinkage-ryū adept, Ujii Yashirō, for instance, does not appear in the *Bushū denraiki*, while the encounter with the Takenouchi-ryū practitioner Takagi Umanosuke cannot be found in the *Bukōden*. By thus complementing each other's lacuna, the two works together provide many of the scenes that make up the fascinating tapestry of Musashi's life.

Both the *Bukōden* and the *Bushū denraiki*, then, have much to offer to a modern reader interested in the life and character of this medieval Japanese swordsman. They give a unique—and to the Western reader totally new—insight in the man Musashi and the way in which he, his exploits, and his heritage were perceived by his immediate successors. It is a happy characteristic of these early historical works that they tell their story not in the clinical and detached tone of modern day academic prose, but in the vernacular of men who were passionate about their subject, but with a simple honesty that still makes for a fascinating read.

☯ The History of the *Bukōden*

Toyoda Hikobei Masanaga was born in 1706, in the village of Yatsushiro, in the province of Higo. He was the oldest son of Toyoda Masatake, a retainer to Nagaoka (Matsui) Naoyuki, the master of Yatsushiro castle.

The Nagaoka were an important clan on the island of Kyushu. Ever since Naoyuki's ancestors had joined forces with the

Hosokawa in the Battle of Sekigahara they had been the chief vassals of the Hosokawa, the clan so closely associated with the duel on Ganryū island and the last years of Musashi's life. Yatsushiro castle lay some twenty miles south along the coast from Kumamoto castle, the imposing headquarters of the Hosokawa clan since 1632. Kumamoto, too, was inextricably linked to the great swordsman. It had been at Kumamoto, after all that, on the invitation of Hosokawa Tadatoshi (1586–1641), Musashi decided to spend the last years of his life. And it had been in the hushed quietude of the nearby Reigan cave that, on the request of Tadatoshi's son, Mitsunao, Musashi had written his now famous *Book of Five Rings*.

Through their connection with the Hosokawa, the history of the Nagaoka clan was closely connected to that of Miyamoto Musashi. Yet it was not merely their vassalage to the Hosokawa clan that gave the successive lords of Yatsushiro castle reason for their affinity with the master swordsman. Naoyuki's grandfather, Nagaoka Okinaga (1582–1661), had been a close friend of Musashi when both men had still been in their forties. Indeed, among the prized possessions of the Nagaoka clan were a number of letters to Okinaga in the accomplished hand of the great swordsman.

Given that history, it was not surprising that Hosokawa Tadatoshi appointed Okinaga's son, Yoriyuki, to look after the old man's needs when, toward the end of his life, Musashi chose to settle in Kumamoto. Okinaga, after all, was by now himself in his sixties and unable to commute between Yatsushiro and Kumamoto with the same ease as his son. Yoriyuki was a keen practitioner of the Taisha-ryū, a school of swordsmanship founded by Marume Nagayoshi (1540–1629), a one-time pupil of the great Kamiizumi Ise no Kami Nobutsuna (1508–77), the founder of the Shinkage-ryū. By the time Musashi retired to Kumamoto, Yoriyuki had become lord of Yatsushiro castle and one of Tadatoshi's chief councilors. Tadatoshi's decision, then, to appoint such an important retainer to serve as Musashi's aide was clear proof of his reverence for the swordsman.

It seems that Yoriyuki acquitted himself of his task with great dedication. He soon won the confidence of the aging swordsman, becoming one of the last students to study the Niten Ichi school of swordsmanship under the great master himself. It is also borne out by the correspondence between Yoriyuki and Musashi's one surviving adoptive son, Iori, who wrote a letter to Yoriyuki saying:

> My father Musashi has fallen ill yet you are looking after him with great care. I am deeply grateful for this and would like to visit you in person, but my commitments here prevent me from doing so. My sincere apologies for this. Thanking you once again, I commend my father to your care.

By the time Masanaga was born, Musashi had already been dead sixty-one years. Hosokawa Tadatoshi, too, had passed away, and so had Nagaoka Okinaga and his adoptive son Yoriyuki. The present lord of Yatsushiro castle was Yoriyuki's natural grandson and heir, Nagaoka Tameyuki, while the Hosokawa clan was now led by Hosokawa Tsunatoshi.

The Toyoda had been favored by fortune since Masanaga's great grandfather, Takahisa, a warrior from Buzen, had been taken on by the Nagaoka a century before on a stipend of a mere thirteen *koku*, especially so under Masanaga's father, Toyoda Masatake (1672–1749). After entering the service of the Nagaoka in 1688 at the age of seventeen as a messenger, he steadily advanced in rank. At the age of twenty he became the clan's chief archivist, and by the time Masanaga was born, he had climbed to the important position of *sakuji bugyō*, the administrator responsible for building and repairs.

With a small fief of one hundred *koku* the Toyoda were no high-flyers yet were respected and reasonably well off.

Even though they now lived in a time of peace, the Toyoda remained keen practitioners of the martial arts. They were, after all, a clan with a martial tradition that went back for many generations. Masanaga's distant ancestor, Toyoda Kagetoshi, a warrior from the Kantō region, had fought under the great Minamoto Yoritomo during the Gempei War (1180–85). Honoring that proud tradition, Masatake applied himself to the martial arts. He was a keen horseman who, like has father, had studied the art according to the Yorisuke school of equestrianism. Needless to say, he was also a swordsman. He had studied Musashi's Niten Ichi-ryū, chiefly under Dōke Munenari, who had acquired his knowledge from none other than Terao Motomenosuke Nobuyuki (1621–88), a direct disciple of the great master himself. Masatake's zest in his pursuits soon bore fruit. In 1728, at the age of fifty-six, he was made the personal tutor in the art of the Niten Ichi-ryū to Nagaoka Tameyuki's son, Toyoyuki.

The young Masanaga, then, grew up in a clan in which the martial arts were pursued with a great degree of zeal—a clan that passed Musashi's heritage on from one generation to the next as if it concerned the family heirloom. Though his father had not known Musashi, his grandfather had, while both Dōke Munenari father and his teacher, Terao Nobuyuki, had been among the master's disciples. As Masanaga grew up his father regaled him with tales of Musashi's exploits, his character, and the circumstances under which he had come to Kumamoto and written the *Book of Five Rings*. These stories, passed down through three generations of Niten Ichi-ryū practitioners and told during long winter evenings, must have inspired Masanaga to learn more about the man who had become his hero—an ambition only fanned by his later visits to the Reigan cave and the monument Iori had erected at

Kokura half a century earlier. It was from a close and knowledgeable source, then, that Masanaga was able to draw when he set out to write his biography of Miyamoto Musashi, especially where it concerned the last few years of the swordsman's eventful life.

The oral traditions of the local warrior clans were not the only source on which Masanaga was able to draw. First of all, of course, there was Musashi's *Book of Five Rings*, as well as his other writings, copies of which were passed on from generation to generation by the Hosokawa clan. Then there were Musashi's letters to Nagaoka Okinaga, which were still in the possession of the Nagaoka family. The Toyoda, too, had its fair share of documents. In his zeal to better understand the great master, Masanaga's father had amassed a veritable treasure trove of information, including a copy of Musashi's introduction to the *Book of Five Rings*, several documents passed on by Terao Nobumasa (Nobuyuki's brother), as well as a number of Musashi's works of art.

There were other, even more important, written sources on which Masanaga was able to draw. From passages in the *Bukōden* it is clear that the author had read (though not always accurately interpreted) the *Kokura hibun*, the epitaph on Iori's monument written by the monk Akiyama Wanao, one of Musashi's closest friends in old age. He had also managed to lay his hands on a copy of the *Honchō bugei shoden*. Written in 1715 by Hinatsu Shigetaka, these "Short Tales on the Martial Arts of Japan," were an important source, as they included an account of the famous duel on Ganryū island.

And what of the *Bushū denraiki*, that first great biography of Musashi's life? Given the proximity of the Fukuoka and Kumamoto domains, it is possible that Masanaga may at least have heard of Tanji Hōkin's biography of Musashi. Yet even if he had known of its existence, it is highly unlikely that he would have been able to read it. The warrior clans in his day were keen to keep their advantage over their rivals and guarded their secrets with a jealousy that bordered on paranoia, especially where they concerned the martial arts.

Masanaga was not alone in embarking on this formidable task. In 1707, one year after Masanaga's birth, his father had completed a work called *Heihō shojosho*, a short treatise on the Niten Ichi school of swordsmanship. It had been with a view to further his research that Masatake had collected the many valuable documents in his possession. The *Heihō shojosho*, however, was not so much concerned with Musashi's life as with the preservation of his heritage, the techniques of the Niten Ichi-ryū. Now it fell to Masanaga to expand on his father's work and, albeit unwittingly, find the pieces in the puzzle of Musashi's life that Hōkin had not yet found.

Masanaga was thirty-three when, in the summer of 1749, his father passed away after a short illness. Being the oldest son, Masanaga succeeded his father as fencing instructor to the Nagaoka clan and became the new head of the Toyoda household in Yatsushiro. Sifting through the huge collection of scrolls, writings, and artwork in his father's library, Masanaga discovered the *Heihō shojosho*, and it was there and then, as he was coming to terms with the death of his father who had been his great inspiration, that the young man decided to honor Masatake's memory by continuing his work and writing a biography on Miyamoto Musashi.

Over the next years Masanaga worked on his life's work, interviewing old practitioners of the Niten Ichi-ryū, gathering and reading every last scrap of text he could find, and visiting the places so closely connected to Musashi's life: the house at Kumamoto where he had lived, the Reigan cave where he had meditated, and the monument at Kokura with his epitaph. Finally, in the spring of 1755, his work was completed. He gave it the title *Bukōden*, the *Official Records of Miyamoto Musashi*.

Masanaga laid down his responsibilities in June 1772, leaving them to his thirty-two-year-old son Kagehide, hoping to spend his last years in quiet retirement to improve on his life's work. But only a few months later, in October of the same year, he suddenly passed away at the age of sixty-six.

Kagehide proved an able and pious son, instructing his lord in the art of fencing according to the Niten Ichi-ryū, and studying Musashi's life as recorded in his father's *Bukōden*. He knew of his father's secret ambition to expand on his original work, and it was not long after that Kagehide made up his mind to fulfill his father's dream and perfect the *Bukōden*. He had, however, noticed that his father's labored and uncompromising style of writing had given rise to a number of misunderstandings, and it was with a view to improve on his father's work and make it more accessible to his followers that Kagehide decided to completely rewrite the *Bukōden*.

Finally, in 1776, four years after his father had passed away, Kagehide completed his work. He gave it the title *Nitenki*. It is a mark of Kagehide's success in achieving his objective that the *Nitenki* is still the most widely known of all the eighteenth century Miyamoto Musashi *denki*.

The *Nitenki*, however, is not necessarily a more accurate work than the *Bukōden*. Though wider in scope and more accessible in prose, the *Nitenki* is clearly the product of a next generation and in many aspects yet a step farther removed from those who had stood near the source. Part of this was simply the product of time, but the author also had a deliberate hand in this. Sources whom his father had mentioned by name were to become anonymous in Kagehide's work. And while the young author did indeed manage to expand on his father's work, many of the sources on whom he based these accounts were of dubious origin, to say the least—a decision that was to lead to the inevitable errors. Thus it holds that at the time of his famous duel with Musashi on Ganryū island,

Sasaki Kojirō was only eighteen years old, while at the same time claiming that he had studied the art of swordsmanship under Toda Seigen, a swordsman born in 1519, almost a century before the duel took place.

The *Bukōden*, then, still remains the foremost source in the Higo strand of the Musashi narrative tradition. It was true that Masanaga was already one generation farther removed from Musashi than Tanji Hōkin, yet the important work done by his father, Masatake (who knew the men who had studied the art of fencing under the great swordsman), ensured that the *Bukōden* manages to maintain that same vital link to the past found in the *Bushū denraiki*. As a consequence, the *Bukōden* has a vitality and authenticity of voice that is only matched by the *Bushū denraiki*, still the chief Chikuzen strand in the fascinating narrative of Miyamoto Musashi.

❧ The Text of the *Bukōden*

Such, then, is the history of the *Bukōden* and its spin-off the *Nitenki*. Sadly, as is the case with Tanji Hōkin's *Bushū denraiki*, no copy in Toyoda Masanaga's hand has survived the ravages of time. The one version that survives was copied by a man by the name of Tamura Hideyuki in the summer of 1819, some two decades after the author of the *Bukōden* had passed away. It is now kept at the Bokudō Library in Kumamoto, which is in the possession of the Tominaga family.

The original text is recorded on two scrolls. The text of each scroll is divided into paragraphs, each on a different episode or aspect of Musashi's life, and each marked with the character "one," as was often done in Masanaga's days. The first scroll consists of thirty-three paragraphs, the second scroll of twenty-seven. As with Hōkin's *Bushū denraiki*, there is the occasional leap back and forth in time, but on the whole the paragraphs of both scrolls are chronologically ordered. Those of the first scroll describe Musashi's life from his early childhood to his death in 1645. The second scroll, by contrast, contains an apparently far more random collection of entries, which may well have served to make up for lacuna in the first text, and is chiefly concerned with Musashi's life at Kumamoto.

Masanaga's work is more that just a biography of Musashi's life. Interspersed throughout the text are direct quotations from other texts, among them the full text of the *Kokura hibun*, giving the reader a direct insight into the kind of sources on which Masanaga drew for his *denki*.

Like the original, the translation consists of two parts. To make the work more accessible (which was, after all, one of the chief reasons for Masanaga's son to write his less accurate *Nitenki*), a few minor modifications have been made to the text. Adhering to the general structure of the *Bukōden*, each chapter is subdivided along the general paragraph structure laid down by Masanaga in his original work, while chapters and subchapters have been given titles where the original text carries none. For the same reasons some alterations have been made in the order of the subchapters. Thus the passages about the banquet, Lord Yoriyuki's inquiry, and the tense conversation between Musashi and his fellow swordsman Shimizu Hōki have been taken from the end of the first scroll and inserted where they really belong, alongside Masanaga's description of Musashi's life in Higo.

A point to keep in mind is that Masanaga records events according to the Japanese, lunisolar calendar. Adapted from the Chinese system of keeping time, the calendar was based on the moon's cycle of 29.5 days with months assigned either twenty-nine or thirty days. This, however, caused a discrepancy between the calendar months and the seasons, so that, every few years, an additional month (*uruzuki*) was inserted to produce years with thirteen months. It is made all the more complex by the Japanese tradition of beginning a new Era (*nengō*) following the death of an emperor, a major calamity, or an auspicious event. This method of keeping time can lead to some confusion, particularly among Western readers, as the Japanese day, date, and year all fail to correspond to the Gregorian calendar. Thus, going by his lunisolar calendar, Masanaga records that Musashi died on May 19 in the second year of Shōhō. According to the Gregorian calendar, however, the swordsman passed away on June 13, 1645. For historical interest, here, Masanaga's dating has been preserved, but to aid the Western reader Western dates have been added in brackets throughout the text.

Another aspect of medieval Japanese literature that may lead to confusion is the way in which people are named. Names are one of the least consistent factors in medieval Japanese texts. Birth, coming of age, succession, profession, high office, retirement, and death all had to find their expression in a person's name, and there are few, if any, persons of any significance in medieval Japan who went through life under one single name. Musashi himself is a case in point. Like the author of the *Bushū denraiki*, at the outset of his biography, Masanaga introduces his subject as Shinmen Musashi no Kami Genshin. In this Masanaga closely follows Musashi's own example, for in his prologue to *The Book of Five Rings* Musashi introduces himself as Shinmen Musashi no Kami Fujiwara no Genshin. It is clear why Musashi did so. Shinmen, the clan into which his father had married, was an ancient breed of warriors who had been involved in Emperor Godaigo's (1288–1339) failed attempt to restore powers to the throne. That involvement had led to exile, an exile from which they were eventually allowed to return and resume their role under the name of Shinmen, or "newly absolved." Genji is an even more straightforward, though perhaps less justified example. As one of the oldest warrior clans in Japan the Genji (or Minamoto, according to a more Japanese read-ing) loomed large on the horizon of the medieval warrior. Their epic struggle with the Heike (or Taira) in the Genpei War (1180–85) — a struggle they won — had swept away the effeminate world of the Heian nobility to make place for a world of martial rule that lasted more than six centuries. Living at the very height of this tradition, there were few warriors in Musashi's days who could resist the temptation to claim some line of descent from one or other illustrious clan, however tenable.

Finally, in the face of impending death, Musashi had to address another important aspect of his life as a warrior: how to assess his life's accomplishments and find peace with his own mortality. Both the *Bukōden* and the *Bushū denraiki* men-tion that, shortly before his death Musashi took the spiritu-al name of Niten Dōraku, which may be crudely translated as the "Niten dilettante."

Japanese names in themselves are often difficult enough to distinguish from each other, let alone remember. So as not to further confuse matters, most characters in the text are identified by their common names, and not, as Masanaga often does, by their long titles of office or posthumous names.

It is to Masanaga's great credit that the man that arises from the pages off the *Bukōden* is far more human that many a modern-day adaptation would suggest. Ultimately, and almost in spite of Musashi's unparalleled skill with the sword, his larger than life stature, he is still a human being, afflict-ed by the same setbacks, torments, and shortcomings to which all of us are prone.

The *Bukōden*
first scroll

Musashi's Early Years

Master Shinmen Musashi Fujiwara Genshin

Master Shinmen Musashi no Kami Fujiwara Genshin devoted himself to the Way of *heihō* from a young age. In many provinces and at various occasions he engaged in numerous contests with the sword and the *bokutō*, facing *heihōsha* who were known throughout the realm, but not once did he fail to claim victory. All this took place from his thirteenth to his twenty-ninth year. However, when he turned thirty and looked back over the previous years, he realized that he had not won because of his own excellence in the art of *heihō*. The workings of the Way being what they are, these victories had been achieved either because he had quite accidentally adhered to the heavenly principles, or because of shortcomings in the schools of fencing practiced by those he had met in duel. It was only at the age of fifty, having applied himself to the art from dawn till dusk for twenty years, that he truly found the Way in the art of *heihō*. From that moment onward was able to spend his days without having look for the Way any longer.

Relying on the principles of *heihō*, everything became clear to Musashi, in whatever art or craft he chose to immerse himself. At this stage Musashi founded the school of two swords and gave it the name of Jissō Enman no Heihō Seikyo Fuzetsu Niten Ichi-ryū.

- Together with the rest of this passage, Musashi's formal name of Shinmen Musashi no Kami Fujiwara Genshin has clearly been taken from the *Book of Five Rings*.
- It is almost certain that Masanaga based his lengthy name for Musashi's school of swordsmanship on the title of the *Kokura hibun*, the epitaph found on the monument Iori had erected for his adoptive father near Kokura in 1654. The epitaph itself is believed to have been written by Akiyama Wanao, the monk whom Musashi had befriended during the last year of his life. Wanao was the abbot of the Taishōji, family temple of the Hosokawa clan in Kumamoto, the place where Musashi spent the last days. The full, strongly Buddhist inspired, title of the *Kokura hibun* runs: "Tengyō Jissō Enman no Heihō Seikyo Fuzetsu," which may be rendered in English as "The Eternal and Truly Divine Manifestation of the Art of Swordsmanship." Outside Wanao, however, Masanaga is the only author to use these terms and it is safe to assume that the majority of Musashi's followers referred to his school of swordsmanship as the Niten Ichi-ryū.

❦ Musashi's Birth and his Various Names

Musashi was a member of the Akamatsu clan from Harima. The Akamatsu were of noble descent, but out of modesty he had taken on the name of Miyamoto, although in his writings on martial arts he did not shy away from using the name Akamatsu.

Musashi was born in the second month of the twelfth year of Tenshō [March 1584]. His infant name was Bennosuke. In old age he came to the province of Higo, where he studied the Buddhist scriptures at the Taishō temple under Akiyama Wanao and took on the spiritual name of Niten Dōraku.

- Being a native of Higo, Masanaga was poorly informed of Musashi's past, connected as it was to the distant province of Harima. Musashi belonged to the Shinmen clan. His father, whose real name was Hirata Munisai, who in his youth had been a senior vassal to the Shinmen, an important warrior clan in the province of Mimasaka. It was from the Shinmen that Munisai had taken his first wife, Omasa, and thereby acquired the clan's name. Omasa was the daughter of Shinmen Munisada, whose ancestors had married into the Akamatsu clan. Musashi, however, was born to Munisai's second wife, Yoshiko. She too descended from the Akamatsu, though it is not clear if she was directly related to Munisai's first wife. Masanaga is not alone in making the link between Musashi and the Akamatsu clan. Tanji Hōkin, the author of the *Bushū denraiki*, similarly claims that Musashi descended from the Akamatsu.
- In keeping with feudal tradition, Musashi's family name of Miyamoto derived from his family's place of descent, a hamlet along the Inaba Kaidō, the inland route that connected the castle town of Himeji to that of Tottori, on the Sea of Japan.

☯ Shinmen Muninosuke and Yoshioka Kenpō

Musashi's father was Shinmen Muninosuke Nobutsuna, the founder of the art of fighting with two swords as well as the *jitte*. They say that he named it the Tōri-ryū.

At that time the greatest warrior in the realm was considered to be Yoshioka Atsusaemon Kenpō, a resident of Kyoto and a private fencing instructor to shogun Ashikaga Yoshiaki (1537–97). On orders of the shogun, a *shiai* was arranged between the two men. It was to be a bout in three rounds. The first round went to Kenpō, the second and third to Muni. And thus the title of *heihōsha* Without Equal Under the Heavens went to Muni.

Later in life, Kenpō had an argument during the festivities to celebrate the completion of the Great Buddha at the Hōkō temple in Kyoto. In the fighting that ensued some eight men found their end under the blade of his sword. Fearing the consequences, he tried to flee the scene by climbing over a mud wall. However, the skirt of his *hakama* got caught on a nail on top of the wall, causing him to fall back on the *yari* of the assembled guards and lose his life. From then on, down to the present day, all men are forbidden to wear swords during imperially sponsored functions.

- The Yoshioka clan in Musashi's days was a clan renowned for its skill with the sword. Their school of swordsmanship, the Yoshioka-ryū, was founded by Yoshioka Naomoto, a merchant in dyed goods who had been trained in the Kyohachi school of swordsmanship and rose to private fencing instructor to the twelfth Ashikaga shogun Ashikaga Yoshiharu (1511–50). The success of the Yoshioka clan reached its zenith under Naomoto's younger brother, Naomitsu, who established the Heihōsho, a martial arts school in the capital's Imadegawa district. It is believed that the man who faced Musashi's father in duel was Naomoto's grandson, Yoshioka Naokata, fencing instructor to the fifteenth Ashikaga shogun Ashikaga Yoshiaki (1537–97). Confusingly, the spiritual name of Kenpō, first adopted by Naomoto, seems to have been inherited by three of his successors, making it difficult to establish the identity of Munisai's adversary with absolute certainty.
- The *jitte* is a traditional weapon that was introduced to Japan during the early Muromachi Period (1333–1568).

It consists of an iron rod that may vary in length between thirty centimeters to a meter. The *jitte* is a defensive weapon in that it is used to deflect an attack with a sword by stopping its downward thrust by means of a fork-like extension situated just above the hilt.

❷ Arima Kihei and Akiyama of Tajima

Musashi inherited his father's tradition of fighting with the *jitte* and the two swords but excelled him in both. In the first year of Keichō [1596], when he reached the age of thirteen, he had a duel with the Shintō-ryū adept Arima Kihei and defeated him.

In the spring of the fourth year of Keichō [1599], he beat a powerful warrior from the province of Tajima by the name of Akiyama. At that time he was sixteen years of age.

• Not much is known about the first warrior to fall victim to Musashi's precocious ability with the sword. Though Masanaga claims that Kihei came from Harima, the line of the Arima clan from which the swordsman descended probably hailed from Hizen, a province on the southern island of Kyushu. So much, at least, is borne out by the *Bushū den-raiki*, which describes the duel in great detail. It claims that Kihei was wearing a so-called *karusan*, a Japanese *haka-ma* modeled after the *calção*, the balloon trousers worn by the Portuguese sailors who reached Kyushu during the middle of the sixteenth century. Unlike traditional *hakama*, the *karusan* had trouser legs that tapered toward the lower end so that they sat tight round the lower shins. They were worn by all kinds of classes, but they were particularly liked by those who spent much time on the road, especially itinerant warriors, who appreciated their wide and comfortable legs, while the narrow ends prevented one from slipping over one's own garment.

How Kihei came to practice the Shinto school of swordsmanship is also not clear. The Shintō-ryū had its roots in the Kantō region. It was founded by Iizasa Chōisai Ienao, a warrior from Sawara in Shimōsa, who developed the old fencing techniques that were preserved at the local shrine of Katori into a comprehensive school of swordsmanship, the Katori Shinto-ryū. Chōisai's heritage was continued by Matsumoto Bizen no Kami Masanobu and propagated by the legendary Tsukahara Bokuden, both practitioners of the Kashima Shinto-ryū, which was centered around the shrine of Kashima in Hitachi. Tsukahara Bokuden traveled throughout the length and breadth of the country, and it was due to these peregrinations that, by the end of the sixteenth century, the Shinto-ryū had become one of the most widely practiced schools of swordsmanship in Japan — so much so that it would even have reached the remote island of Kyushu. One of the Arima clan members, a certain Arima Yamato no Kami Kenshin, is said to have studied the Kashima Shinto school of swordsmanship under Matsumoto Masanobu, while his son Tokisada was to become a fencing instructor to Tokugawa Ieyasu.

- The Akiyama clan had taken on the name of the area in the province of Kai where they settled during the twelfth century. They descended from the Seiwa Genji and were closely related to the famous Takeda clan, whose notorious offspring, Takeda Shingen, played such an important role during the Warring States period (1469–1573). With the final defeat of Shingen's son Katsuyori at the hands of Oda Nobunaga in 1582, however, the Akiyama clan, too, went under and lost all of its domains. The warrior Musashi encountered may well have been one of the clan's survivors who roamed the country, as did so many other *rōnin*.

❷ Musashi and the Battle of Sekigahara

In June of the fifth year of Keichō [August 1600], the quelling of Fushimi castle.

In August of the same year [September 1600], the siege of Gifu castle.

On September 15 of the same year [October 21, 1600], the Battle of Sekigahara.

Akamatsu Sahyōei no Kami Hiromichi passes away.

- The vexing brevity and almost willful ambiguity of this passage seems to illustrate how poorly informed Masanaga was about Musashi's early military career. What is meant by "the quelling of Fushimi castle"? Is Masanaga suggesting that Musashi actually participated in the siege of Fushimi castle? This would mean that Musashi fought under the command of Ishida Mitsunari, who laid siege to the castle on August 27, 1600. What, also, was Musashi's connection to the siege of Gifu castle? And did he really participate in the Battle of Sekigahara?

  If Masanaga is indeed suggesting that Musashi somehow took part in all of these events, he is making a poor case. Fushimi castle, after all, was besieged by the western forces. Indeed, it was the siege of Fushimi castle that gave Tokugawa Ieyasu the pretext to convene with his allies in the northern town of Oyama on September 2 and make plans for a final confrontation between his forces and those of his adversary, Ishida Mitsunari. And it was in the run-up to that confrontation on the plains of the old barrier of Sekigahara that, on September 28, Ieyasu's troops laid siege of Gifu castle. In other words, if Musashi did indeed participate both in the siege of Fushimi castle and that of Gifu castle, he would have had to change sides within the space of only one month, which would have made him a bit of a turncoat, to say the least.

The key to this obscure passage probably lies in its last sentence. Akamatsu Sahyōe no Kami Hiromichi, better known as Akamatsu Hirohide (1562–1600), was the second son of Akamatsu Masahiro, the master of Tatsuno castle in the province of Harima. Following the successive deaths of his father and brother, Hirohide became a lord in his own right but with Toyotomi Hideyoshi's conquest of the western provinces during the seventies he lost most of his lands in Harima. Accepting the new status quo, over the next few years, Hirohide he fought hard on behalf of Hideyoshi, first at Komaki (1583) and then at Nagakute (1583). In reward for his services he received a fief of well over twenty thousand *koku* in the province of Tajima, with Takeda castle as his new headquarters. Being from the western provinces, he chose to side with Ishida Mitsunari, but at the time of the Battle of Sekigahara he changed sides by crossing into the neighboring province of Inaba and attacking Tottori castle. In the clampdown that followed after the dust had settled, Ieyasu ordered him to commit ritual suicide.

With Hirohide's death, the last line of the Akamatsu clan had died out, and it is here that we should probably seek the significance of these few elusive lines. As Masanaga states in the outset of his work, Musashi was a descendant (through his mother's side) from the Akamatsu, and the death of the last scion of this old and illustrious clan would have been of great relevance to the personal history of a swordsman in a fuedal society obsessed with pedigree.

It is tempting, finally, to think that these lines were written, not by Masanaga, but by his father, Masatake, short notes on important historical events jotted down in passing in his *Heihō shojoshō*, in the awareness that these events needed further inquiry in the context of his research. It seems that neither Masatake nor Masanaga was able or willing to explore them any further. If they had, they would have discovered that these epoch-making events never directly impinged on Musashi's life. Indeed, perhaps Masanaga did pursue these lines of inquiry, only to find that his hero did not play a role in them. Constrained on the one hand by his reluctance to disclose his discovery, yet compelled by his piety toward his father to honor the integrity of the latter's research, he probably decided to compromise and simply take these lines over in his own work and leave it at that.

- The *Bukōden*'s reticence about Musashi's early life stands in sharp contrast with the great detail with which this episode in Musashi's life is described in the *Bushū denraiki*. It is safe to assume, therefore, that, when the Battle of Sekigahara was raging on the island of Honshu, Musashi was down in Kyushu, fighting alongside the eastern forces of Kuroda Yoshitaka (1546–1604) in the sieges of Aki and Tomiku castles.

Musashi's Coming of Age

Duels With Members of the Yoshioka Clan

In the ninth year of Keichō [1604], when he was twenty-one years old, Musashi went up to Kyoto, where he met with members of the Yoshioka clan, who were said to be "The Foremost *Heihōsha* in Japan." Many times he dueled with them, but not once was he defeated.

The first duel was with Yoshioka Seijūrō [Naoshige], the legitimate heir of Yoshioka Kenpō. It was fought on the grounds of the Rendai temple. Seijūrō fought with a *shinken*. Musashi was armed with a *bokutō*, and struck out once. Seijūrō collapsed and lost consciousness. He was saved in that they had agreed only to attack once. The Yoshioka *deshi* placed him on a stretcher and took him home where they nursed him back to health. In the end, he abandoned the martial life and took the tonsure.

However, afterward, Seijūrō's younger brother, Denshichirō, left Kyoto to meet Musashi in a duel. He charged at Musashi, brandishing a *bokutō* of some five feet in length. But Musashi instantly disarmed him and struck him down there and then. Denshichirō fell down where he stood and expired.

The Yoshioka and their followers were now consumed with hatred and Seijūrō's son, Matashichirō, gathered his disciples outside the city at Kudarimatsu feigning to practice, but there were several hundreds of them, all armed with sticks, bows, and arrows, for they wished to kill Musashi. But Musashi saw through the ambush. He killed Matashichirō and dispersed his followers, and having displayed his supremacy, he returned to Kyoto. As a result, the house of Yoshioka ceased to exist.

After that Musashi visited many places throughout the country, meeting with *heihōsha* of different schools. He engaged in some sixty *shiai*, but not once was he defeated. All this came to pass between his thirteenth and his twenty-ninth year.

The above are excerpts taken from the *Kokura hibun* and the *Book of Five Rings.*

- The Yoshioka clan in Musashi's days was renowned for its skill with the sword. Yoshioka Seijūrō Naoshige was a descendant of the famous Yoshioka Naomoto, a merchant in dyed goods who had been trained in the Kyohachi school of swordsmanship. Naomoto, better known by his spiritual name of Kenpō, developed his own style of fencing, called the Yoshioka-ryū, and became the private fencing instructor to the twelfth Ashikaga shogun Yoshiharu (1511–50).

  The success of the Yoshioka clan reached its zenith under Kenpō's younger brother, Naomitsu, who established the Heihōsho, a martial arts school in Kyoto's Imadegawa district. Naomitsu's descendants (three of whom confusingly inherited Naomoto's spiritual name of Kenpō) continued to serve the Ashikaga house as fencing instructors, down to the fifteenth Ashikaga shogun Ashikaga Yoshiaki (1537–97).

  In 1573, however, the fortunes of the Yoshioka clan took a turn for the worst, when Oda Nobunaga, vexed by the shogun's collusion with his arch-enemy Takeda Shingen (1521–73), sent Yoshiaki into exile. The Yoshioka clan continued to practice their school of swordsmanship, but its close association with the Ashikaga house meant that it would never again enjoy the degree of esteem it had known under Naomitsu.

- Most sources agree that there was a duel between Musashi and one or more members of the Yoshioka clan. Even the skirmish with the huge number of Yoshioka *deshi* is mentioned in various other sources, although all vary in their accounts of the incident, giving rise to heated arguments. One of these evolves round the actual place where the skirmish took place. Following the *Kokura hibun*, both the *Bushū denraiki* and the *Bukōden* specify the place as Kudarimatsu, a vexingly elusive designation as there are many places in and around Kyoto that are historically associated with the name.

❷ To Face Things Without Changing One's Heart

Dōke Heizō Munenari was a *deshi* of Musashi's direct pupil, Terao Motomenosuke Nobuyuki, and a retainer of Hosokawa Tsunatoshi. His father, Kakusaemon, too, had been one of Musashi's *deshi*.

According to Kakusaemon Musashi would say:

It is truly difficult not to change one's heart when one faces danger. Long ago I met with Yoshioka Matashichirō in a duel at Kudarimatsu (a grove near the village of the Ichijō temple). All my students said: "Matashichirō sees you as the enemy of his father and uncle. Surely, he will bring along a large number of followers and ambush you in a pincer attack so as to avenge himself for what you have done to his brother Sejūrō. You are throwing yourself into the jaws of death, for this is a truly dangerous situation. Please let us accompany you and fight them together." But I said: "That will not do. To go in with a large number of my followers and join in battle is tantamount to forming a faction and raising an army. The shogunate has issued a decree strictly forbidding such things. I must observe these injunctions. I would feel guilty if any of you were to join me."

Come to think of it, the military tactics of the Yoshioka clan were not something to be greatly feared. When I met Matashichirō's father, Seijūrō [Naoshige], and his uncle, Denshichirō, in a duel, I was late and won. Therefore, this time round, I decided to take the reverse course and left Kyoto before dawn.

On my way there I passed in front of the Hachiman shrine, and I thought to myself: "What good fortune that I should come before the gods by accident. I should seize this opportunity and pray for victory." When I went up to the shrine's altar and took the crimson cord to sound the temple gong it suddenly occurred to me that I had never before put any faith in gods and Buddha. However, now, as I was facing imminent danger, I was suddenly eager to pay my respects. "Ah," I realized, "I must be flinching from danger!" At that moment I let loose the temple gong's cord and stepped down from the altar. I was so deeply ashamed that I felt the sweat running down by back.

I immediately set out running and arrived at Kudarimatsu. Dawn had not yet arrived, and I waited silently in the shade of the pine trees. After a while Matashichirō arrived with several dozens of followers in his wake carrying torches, and as they approached I could hear him say: "There's no mistaking; he's sure to show up late again and break his promise." At that moment I leaped out of the shade and confronted them shouting: "Musashi has been waiting for you!"

Surprised, Matashichirō drew his sword and rushed toward me at full speed while I awaited him with my sword drawn and ready. Even as he flinched Matashichirō struck, but I moved aside and struck him dead in a single blow with a three-foot *tachi* forged by Ōhara Sanemori.

His followers now all drew their swords and came rushing toward me. Some were even armed with small bows, and one arrow struck my sleeve. But when I suddenly advanced they panicked and scattered in all directions. I had gained complete victory.

Recalling that moment at the Buddhist altar it struck me again how difficult it truly is to not to change one's heart in the face of danger.

In his own works, too, Musashi writes: "Honor the gods and Buddha, but do not ask them any favors." This account by Musashi covers events that occurred between the seventeenth year of Kanei [1640] and the second year of Shōhō [1645].

• Dōke Heizō Munenari belonged to a clan of retainers to the Hosokawa clan. His great-grandfather had entered the service of Hosokawa Tadaoki in 1602, two years after the Battle of Sekigahara. At that time Tadaoki was still the lord of Kokura castle, in the province of Buzen. When Tadaoki was promoted to the fiefdom of Kumamoto the Dōke followed them and were granted a fief of more than two thousand *koku*. When, in old age, Musashi settled in Kumamoto, Munenari's father, Kakusaemon, became one of his last pupils.

- Terao Motomenosuke Nobuyuki (1621–88) was a retainer of Hosokawa Tadatoshi. Along with his brother, Terao Magonojō Nobumasa (1611–72), he became one of the three men selected by Musashi to keep the Niten Ichi school of swordsmanship alive.

- Masanaga's description of the encounter with Yoshioka Matashichirō is somewhat at odds that of Hōkin in the *Bushū denraiki*. Though both authors pit Musashi against Yoshioka Matashichirō, according to Hōkin, Musashi at first encourages his followers to stand their ground, pushing one of them forward with the words: "If you slacken your resolve here you will lose your life; remain firm." Only when the young man is struck by an arrow does Musashi take the lead, but he, too, is eventually forced to retreat under the onslaught and flee into the grounds of a nearby temple. In the end, he is only rescued with the help of the *shoshidai*, the deputy governor of the Samurai Dokoro, which policed Kyoto's busy streets.

- The mystery of the location of Kudarimatsu seems resolved by Masanaga's (as well as Hōkin's) mention of the Ichijō temple, which is situated east of Kyoto. The shrine Musashi passed on his way to Kudarimatsu was probably the Hachidai shrine, which is situated only a few hundred meters away from the Ichijō temple.

A possible contender to the Ichijō temple is the Kitano shrine, which is dedicated to Hachiman, the god of war, and situated west of Kyoto, equally close to an area of the city called Kudarimatsu. This should not detract from the fact that Hōkin mentions that Musashi sought refuge in the grounds of a temple and not a shrine. Moreover, both the *Bukōden* and the *Nitenki* explicitly state that the encounter took place at the village of the Ichijō temple.

☻ The Duel on Ganryū Island I

Ganryū Kojirō was a student of Toda Seigen, a generous man by nature and in the prime of his life.

According to the *Honchō bugei shoden*, Toda Seigen's common name was Gorōsaemon and he was born in the village of Jōkyōji, in the province of Echizen. His father, Jibusaemon, and grandfather, Kurōemon, both served the house of Asakura and in those days studied the art of swordsmanship. Then Gorōsaemon fell ill and, taking the tonsure under the name of Seigen, passed the position of family patriarch on to his younger brother, Jibusaemon. Yet he continued to excel in the art of swordsmanship called Chūjō-ryū and even won bouts with a *tantō* of no more than one-and-a-half feet in length.

From a young age Kojirō served Seigen in the role of *uchidachi*. Wielding a *tantō* of one-and-a-half feet, Seigen would win bouts against opponents with swords of three feet in length. But already at this young age, when fighting with the long sword, Kojirō was almost Seigen's equal. And thus, at the age of eighteen, Kojirō left Seigen's service to found his own school of swordsmanship, which he gave the name Gan-ryū.

Kojirō's Gan-ryū was far superior to Seigen's Chūjō-ryū. Traveling the country on his *musha shugyō*, Kojirō visited the province of Buzen. Lord Hosokawa Tadaoki praised the Gan school of swordsmanship and for some time Kojirō stayed at his castle of Kokura.

It was at this juncture that Musashi came down from the capital and stayed at the *yashiki* of Nagaoka Okinaga, who had once been a *deshi* to Musashi's father, Munisai, and said to him: "I hear that Kojirō's art of swordsmanship is exceedingly rare and I would like to meet him in duel. It is only because you were once connected to my father that I now ask that you enable this contest to go forth."

Master Okinaga consented and let Musashi stay under his roof. He immediately submitted a request to Lord Tadaoki's elders, who deliberated on the issue for the next two days. Already the issue had come to Lord Tadaoki's ears, and they decided a day for the contest, which would be held on an isolated island near the port Kokura. (This island was called Mukōjima or Funashima, but now it is also known by the name of Ganryū island. It lies on the border between the provinces of Buzen and Nagato. From Kokura it is close to two-and-a-half miles by boat, and the same from Shimonoseki.) A day before the event, orders were issued throughout the castle town that there was to be no participation or gathering, and these orders were strictly observed.

Master Okinaga now let Musashi know that he was to meet with Kojirō on the island at seven o'clock in the morning, and that Kojirō would be ferried across in one of Lord Tadaoki's boats, while Musashi would cross over to the island in one of Master Okinaga's boats. At this, Musashi whole face lit up with delight, and he was deeply grateful to Master Okinaga for his mediation.

However, on the eve of the event, Musashi suddenly went missing and could not be found anywhere. All of Kokura was searched, but he remained untraceable. At this everyone said: "During his stay here, he must have heard of Ganryū's unparalleled sleight of hand, taken fright and fled!" Master Okinaga, too, was at a loss what to do and, utterly dumbfounded, could do nothing else than regret this unexpected turn of events. At last, in the dead of night, he summoned his men and said: "Considering things carefully, if indeed he has grown scared and fled, why wait until today? He must be up to something. He has already been to Shimonoseki the day before he came here, and maybe he has gone down to Shimonoseki with the intention to cross over to the island from there." Having said this, he immediately sent a messenger to Shimonoseki, and lo and behold, Musashi was indeed at Shimonoseki (where he was staying at the house of the ship's chandler Kobayashi Tarōsaemon).

Turning to the messenger, Musashi said: "I was indeed told that I would be ferried across to the island in one of Master Okinaga's boats, and I am deeply grateful for his Master's kind consideration. However, Kojirō and I are now enemies. Hence, it would be unbecoming if Kojirō were to cross over in a boat of Lord Tadaoki, and I in a boat of Master Okinaga, who, after all, is one of the Lord's vassals. I am deeply grateful to Master Okinaga's for having made my wish come true, but he need not bother about such matters. I realize that I should have told him this in person, but knowing that he would have insisted, I decided to come here without saying anything.

Tomorrow morning I will cross over to Mukōjima island in one of the local boats here, and his lordship can rest assured that I will be there at the appointed hour."

- Though not mentioned once in his own writings, the duel at the island of Funashima is the most famous episode in Miyamoto Musashi's life and has come to epitomize his ingenious fencing skills. Situated in the Shimonoseki straits, the narrow waters between the main island of Honshu and the southern island of Kyushu, the island is still called Funashima, although the historical duel has resulted in the island's second name of Ganryū.

- Hosokawa Tadaoki (1563–1646) was the lord of Kokura castle in Buzen, the most northern province of Kyushu. In the famous Battle of Sekigahara, when a fragmented Japan was again united and brought under central control, Tadaoki had joined the side of the eastern forces, under the control of Tokugawa Ieyasu, founder of the Tokugawa Bakufu. In reward for his valiant services, Tadaoki was awarded with the Kokura fiefdom, with a total revenue of close to four hundred thousand *koku*.

- Nagaoka (Matsui) Okinaga (1582–1661) was a Hosokawa retainer. He was the second son of Nagaoka Yasuyuki, the lord of Kitsuki castle, in the neighboring province of Bungo. In 1600, when Musashi was living with his father in Nakatsu, Kitsuki castle had come under attack of the forces of Ōtomo Yoshimune (1558–1605). Yasuyuki had called on the help of Kuroda Yoshitaka, the lord of Musashi's father. According to the *Bushū denraiki*, Musashi first saw action during the ensuing battle for Tomiku castle. It is not unlikely that it was during this period, when both were in their teens, that Musashi and Okinaga first struck up their friendship. Toyoda Masanaga (the *Bukōden*'s author) claims that Okinaga had once been one of Munisai's *deshi*, which is not unlikely, given that Munisai was an accomplished swordsman.

❷ The Duel on Ganryū Island II

The next morning, when the sun stood already high in the sky, Musashi was still asleep and snoring loudly. And just when his host, Tarōsaemon, came to wake him, the messenger from Kokura again arrived to say that Musashi was late and that the dual had been delayed. Several times more the messenger came round, urgently requesting Musashi to make haste. At long last, Musashi rose from his bed, ate his breakfast, and began to whittle away at an oar he had received from his host, crafting it into a makeshift *bokutō*. The oarsman who ferried him across to the island was one of Tarōsaemon's men.

Finally, at around ten o'clock in the morning, they arrived at Funashima. They moored the boat at a pole on the west side, where the island protruded out several hundred yards and where the shallows were only a few feet deep. Musashi was lying down in the boat, having taken from his belt a hand towel and tying it round his head. He was wearing a lined kimono, its sleeves tucked up with paper strings he had twisted during the crossing, and over it he wore a padded night gown (could it be that under this he was wearing a *karusan hakama*? Some claim that he was wearing a *hakama* of white leather, because it is said that during the dual on Ganryū island his leather *hakama* was cut).

Kojirō by now was exceedingly tired of waiting and was yawning while he stretched himself. When he saw Musashi approach in the distance, he went to the water's edge and called out: "Why is it that you are late while I have already arrived? Is it that you have lost nerve?" But Musashi remained silent and pretended he had not heard him. Instead, he took off the padded garment, tucked the *tantō* into his belt, took his *bokutō*, and waded across the shallows on his bare feet as he raised the trousers of his *hakama*, exposing his shins as he did.

Kojirō was wearing a *karusan hakama* over a bright red, sleeveless *haori* and on his feet he was wearing straw sandals. Drawing his three-feet long sword, Kojirō cast his sheath into the sea and stood at the water's edge, watching as Musashi approached through the shallows. At that point Musashi halted and called out saying: "Kojirō, you've lost! If you had come to conquer, why on earth should you throw your sheath away?" At this Kojirō grew angry and, as Musashi drew near, he struck out at Musashi's brow, cutting the knot in the latter's head towel, which fell to the ground. At the same time, Musashi's oar struck him on the head, and Kojirō fell where he stood. Musashi lowered his oar and stood there for some time before he raised it to strike out again. But Kojirō, who was still lying down, struck out at Musashi's legs, cutting away some three inches of the *hakama* he had tied up above his knees. But already Musashi's oar had struck his opponent in the side, causing his hips to break under the impact and Kojirō to pass out.

After a while Musashi threw away his oar and knelt down beside Kojirō, testing whether he was breating by holding his hand over his nose and mouth. At length he rose, and having briefly bowed to Lord Tadaoki's inspectors, he rose, took up his oar and jumped aboard the waiting boat. (Some say that he was chased off the island by men armed with *yari* and arrows. In my father's records it is written that Musashi jumped the makeshift fence and that the arrows failed to strike home because he boarded the boat.) Then he pushed off and sailed back to the mainland.

Shortly afterward, he came to Kokura and visited Master Okinaga's *yashiki* to seek confirmation of his victory. Again the elders convened, but they could not pronounce a verdict, so that he returned to Shimonoseki. According Tanaka Satafu [Morikage] Musashi even wrote a letter to Master Okinaga following his victory (it is said that Satafu was still a child at this time).

All this was recounted in the summer of the second year of Shōtoku [1712] by a merchant from Kokura (by the name of Muraya Kanpachirō). Kanpachirō had been the oarsman who ferried Musashi across to the island, and it was he who related the events of that day in detail in healthy old age.

- A *karusan* is a Japanese *hakama* modeled after the *calção*, the balloon trousers worn by the Portuguese sailors who reached Kyushu during the middle of the sixteenth century. Unlike traditional *hakama*, the *karusan* had trouser legs that tapered toward the lower end so that they sat tight round the lower shins. They were worn by all kinds of classes, but they were particularly liked by those who spent much time on the road, especially itinerant warriors, who appreciated their wide and comfortable legs, while the narrow ends prevented one from slipping over one's own garment. According to the *Bushū denraiki*, Musashi was indeed wearing a *karusan hakama*.
- A *haori* is a lightweight silk jacket originally meant to be worn by men as a component of the *hakama*.

- Probably as a result of Musashi's reticence on the whole event there are huge discrepancies between the various accounts of what went down on the island of Ganryū. Whereas Masanaga holds that Kojirō was the first to arrive at the island, Tanji Hōkin, the author of the *Bushū denraiki*, claims that it was Musashi who first set foot on the island. Predictably, given the outcome of the bout, either scenario can be made to work in Musashi's favor, according to Hōkin because Musashi can dictate events, according to Masanaga because he caused his opponent to lose patience.

  There are other, more pertinent differences between these two versions of events. While the *Bushū denraiki* claims that the event was witnessed by Hosokawa Tadaoki's son, Tadatoshi (then still lord of Moji castle, northeast of Kokura), the *Bukōden* only makes mention of what are referred to as Lord Tadaoki's *kenshi*, or "inspectors." No mention is made of Tadaoki's son. Instead, Masanaga mentions that some sources claim that Musashi was chased off the island by Hosokawa retainers who were riled by the outcome of the bout. Though these may have been Kojirō's *deshi*, it seems unlikely since, according to Masanaga, Tadaoki had strictly forbidden anyone to observe or participate in the duel.

- Tanaka Satafu Morikage is believed to have been among Musashi's last *deshi*. He was one of Nagaoka Okinaga's retainers, who, like Musashi, had taken part in the suppression of the Shimabara Rebellion and had climbed to considerable rank by the time his master became lord of Yatsushiro castle. Morikage died in 1705, one year before Masanaga was born, so that the author must have taken Morikage's account from his father's writings (to which, incidentally, he refers a few lines earlier in the text). It is not clear to what degree Masanaga based the rest of his account on what his father had learned from Morikage.

Yet, as the author points out, Satafu was still very young when the duel on Ganryū island took place, and while he would have heard a great deal about the event during his lifetime, he can not be considered a true eyewitness.

• Next to nothing is known about Muraya Kanpachirō. Though the author does not explicitly mention it, it is clear that here too Masanaga was drawing from his father's writings, as Masanaga would only have been six in 1712. If, as Masanaga claims, Kanpachirō had been the oarsman who ferried Musashi across to Funashima island, he must indeed have reached a very old age, for by then the duel on Ganryū island already lay a century in the past. A possible explanation is that Masanaga's father recorded the account in 1712 (when he was forty years old), but that he had actually met the merchant when he was much younger).

Musashi in His Prime

Musashi and the Osaka Campaigns

In October of the nineteenth year of Keichō [November 1614], when Musashi was thirty-one, the [winter] campaign against Osaka castle.

On May 8 of the next year, the fall of Osaka castle.

- Vexingly, but not surprisingly, the *Bukōden* is even less forthcoming about Musashi's role in the Osaka campaigns that the *Bushū denraiki*. There is not much the latter adds, either, except for stating that "Musashi took part in the two sieges of Osaka castle and slew many men with his ancestral *naginata*." Neither of the two works reveal on which side and under whom Musashi took part in the siege.
- The two sieges of Osaka castle, both conducted by Tokugawa Ieyasu, were the natural culmination of unresolved contentions in the wake of the Battle of Sekigahara. In 1603 Ieyasu had seized control and founded the Edo Bakufu (1603–1867) by having himself appointed Sei-I Tai Shōgun, or "Barbarian Subduing Generalissimo," and abolishing the *go-tairō*, the Council of Five Regents.

  The council had been called into life in 1598 by Toyotomi Hideyoshi when, from his deathbed, he sought to ensure that he would be succeeded by his son, Hideyori, who was then only five years old. He had stopped short, however, of dealing with Hideyori, as many warlords still looked up to the latter heir as their true overlord. Instead, he sought to contain him and his allies by building and reinforcing a large number of castles throughout the Home Provinces, The largest castle in the region, however, remained Osaka castle. And it was there that Toyotomi Hideyori was allowed to reside and receive visiting vassals. Several attempts were made to reconcile the two houses, but with the successive deaths of their most staunch vassals the house of Toyotomi became increasingly isolated. In their isolation the Toyotomi became increasingly intransigent, giving Ieyasu all the more reason to remove this obstacle to absolute power.

The friction between the two parties came to a head in 1614, when the house of Toyotomi celebrated their reconstruction of the Hōkō temple with an inscription on the temple bell that read "May the state be peaceful and prosperous; in the east it greets the pale moon, and in the west bids farewell to the setting sun." Likening the house of Ieyasu (which had its power base in the eastern provinces) to the moon—and a pale one, at that—and the house of Toyotomi (whose supporters resided chiefly in the western provinces) to the sun, went a step too far for Ieyasu. Having furthermore been informed by his spies that Hideyori was steadily amassing troops at Osaka castle, in the winter of 1614 Ieyasu raised a force of more than one hundred and sixty thousand men and laid siege to the castle.

Osaka castle, however, was a formidable stronghold. Following a period of fierce fighting in which neither made much headway, both parties came to a settlement in which the Toyotomi forces agreed to fill in the castle's outer moat. This was on January 18, 1615. Within only a few months, however, hostilities again erupted when Ieyasu's forces sought also to fill up the inner moat. Taking the initiative, the western forces sought to intercept Ieyasu's forces prior to their arrival, first at Kashi-i, then at the Dōmyō temple, and finally on the doorstep of the Tennō temple, only a few miles south of Osaka castle. At length, however, Hideyori's forces were driven back into the castle, where on June 4, Hideyori recognized defeat by committing ritual suicide. The Osaka winter and summer campaigns, as they came to be known in Japan, put a final and decisive end to the armed resistance against the authority of the Edo Bakufu (1603–1867).

- Though neither the *Bukōden* nor the *Bushū denraiki* reveal on which side and under whom Musashi served in the summer campaign, it is now widely accepted that he did so under the command of Mizuno Katsunari (1564–1651).

Born at Kariya castle, in the province of Mikawa, the lines of Katsunari's clan were closely intertwined with those of the Tokugawa (then still called Matsudaira), who had their headquarters in nearby Okazaki castle. Katsunari's aunt was none other than Ieyasu's mother, making him Ieyasu's direct cousin. Katsunari had made his career in the Tokugawa ranks and had fought in numerous battles under Ieyasu, including the famous battles at Komaki and Nagakute (1584), the only time Ieyasu and Hideyoshi ever confronted each other on the field of battle.

It seems that the young Katsunari was possessed of the same fierce temperament as Musashi, for it was during this battle that the young warrior landed himself in trouble when he killed one of his father's retainers in a fit of anger and he was expelled from Mikawa province for a while. It was partly through the intervention of his cousin, Ieyasu, that relations with his father were restored. Over the following years he continued to serve Ieyasu, most conspicuously so in the run-up to the Battle of Sekigahara, when he distinguished himself in the sieges of the castles of Gifu and Ōgaki. His valor gained him the rank of fifth-level retainer.

Exactly how Katsunari and Musashi met is unclear, but it must have been their similarly fierce disposition that drew the two warriors together. Advanced in years and a man of high rank, Katsunari was very much Musashi's senior, but the great trust he put in the western warrior was revealed when he appointed Musashi as an attendant to his son Katsutoshi.

More proof of the close relation between Musashi and the house of Mizuno came shortly after, when Musashi, who had no sons of his own, adopted the third and fourth son of Nakagawa Shimanosuke, who served Katsunari as *musha bugyō*, the magistrate of warriors.

- Sadly only one record, the *Kirō zatsuroku*, gives an account of Musashi's actions during the siege. Nevertheless, Musashi and his fellow warriors must have acquitted themselves well, for it was in reward for his contribution to Japan's pacification that Katsunari was awarded the large Fukuyama fiefdom in the province of Higo. It was there that in 1619 he began the construction of Fukuyama castle, which would remain headquarters of the Mizuno clan up until the end of the seventeenth century.

❪ Musashi Settles in Kokura

In the ninth year of Kanei [1632] Lord Hosokawa Tadaoki was promoted to the fiefdom of Higo, while Lord Ogasawara Tadazane was promoted to the Kokura fiefdom.

It was in the second year of Kanei [1634] that Musashi, too, came to Kokura. Lord Tadazane treated Musashi with great hospitality, and it was at Kokura that Musashi from then on lived. Musashi at this time was fifty-one years old.

- Ogasawara Tadazane (1596–1667) was the lord of the Akashi fiefdom, in Musashi's ancestral province of Harima. It is not clear when the two first met, but both had fought on the side of the eastern forces during the Osaka campaigns, when both Tadazane's older brother, Tadanaga, and his father, Hidemasa, were killed in action, and the Akashi estate was left to him.

It had been shortly afterward, when Tadazane set about building Akashi castle, that Musashi entered Tadazane's service as an adviser to the *zōei bugyō*, the construction magistrate in charge of the whole project. Recognizing the warrior's artistic qualities Tadazane had also put Musashi personally in charge of the design of the castle gardens and a small tea house.

For more than a decade Musashi remained in Harima, leading a relatively peaceful existence, but that life was uprooted once more when his lord was promoted in rank. In a feudal system in which the Bakufu had no newly conquered territories to distribute, the only way to allot larger territories was through promotion and demotion — a musical chairs with fiefdoms.

This was exactly what happened early in 1632, when Hosokawa Tadatoshi (1586–1641), who had already succeeded his father in 1620, was promoted to the Kumamoto fiefdom in Higo. This meant that the Kokura fiefdom in Buzen was free to be bestowed on someone else who deserved promotion, and it so happened that the Bakufu chose Ogasawara Tadazane to be the new lord of the Kokura fiefdom.

- The *Bukōden* is one of the few sources to shed any light on Musashi's actions immediately after Tadazane's move to Kokurua. The *Bushū denraiki*, too, suggests that Musashi remained in Tadazane's service following the latter's move, since it describes how only five years later, in response to Tadazane's request, he accompanies his son, Nagatsugu, as a guardian during the suppression of the Shimabara Rebellion. This view is also supported by the *Harima kagami*, a topography compiled in 1762 by Hirano Yōsai. Writing about Musashi's adoptive son, Iori, Yōsai mentions how the young man, having entered the service of the Ogasawara at the age of sixteen (in Akashi), "he accompanied the house of his employer when it moved to Kokura in Buzen because he was Musashi's adoptive child."

❷ The Martial Artsman Ujii Yashirō

Before Musashi moved to Higo, a practitioner of martial arts called Ujii Yashirō, a senior and direct pupil of Lord Yagyū Tajima no Kami Munenori, came down to Higo on an errand for his lord. Lord Tadatoshi, incidentally, had once himself been among one of Lord Munenori's *deshi*.

One day, in response to a summons from Lord Tadatoshi, Musashi left Kokura and went down to Higo, for it was his lordship's wish that Musashi and Yashirō have a duel in his presence. Both duelists were made to sign a solemn pledge in which they would desist from criticizing each other's school of swordsmanship. No one else would be present at the event, except for a young page by the name of Urabe Tafu, who bore his lordship's sword, and he too was made to sign a solemn pledge to speak to no one about what he had seen.

Up to three times Musashi dueled with Yashirō, brandishing his *tachi*, but not once was Yashirō able to break through his defense. Given that they were fighting in his lordship's presence, Musashi, on his side, satisfied himself with merely countering Yashirō's attacks, without ever striking out forcefully. Lord Tadatoshi was astonished. He, too, took his place opposite Musashi but equally failed to win even once. From then on Lord Tadatoshi gave up on the Yagyū-ryū and took up practicing Musashi's Niten Ichi-ryū.

- Hosokawa Tadatoshi (1586–1641) is reputed to have been an avid practitioner of the martial arts. According to the *Bushū denraiki*, he attended (and perhaps even arranged) the contest between Musashi and Sasaki Kojirō.
- Munenori was the son of Yagyū Muneyoshi, once the lord of Yagyū castle, in the northeastern part of Yamato province. Muneyoshi was one of the greatest swordsmen of the sixteenth century and became Tokugawa Ieyasu's fencing instructor in 1594 after he had lost his castle and territories in Toyotomi Hideyoshi's land reforms. Both father and son were renowned practitioners of the Yagyū Shinkage school of swordsmanship, a blend of their own Yagyū traditions and the Shinkage school developed by the great Kamiizumi Nobutsuna, who stayed at Yagyū castle during the late 1560s.
- The *"tachi"* with which, according to Masanaga, Musashi is dueling here is a wooden version of the longest of the pair of swords traditionally worn by samurai.

Musashi's Final Years

Musashi Decides to Settle in Higo

Concerning the circumstances under which Musashi came to live in our province of Higo, it seems that this came about as a result of the mediation of Iwama Rokubei [Masanari] (the keeper of Kumamoto castle). In response, Musashi dictated the following letter to Sakazaki Naizen.

To Master Sakazaki Naizen

Through Iwama Rokubei you inquired after my social circumstances. I could, however, not reply orally, so that I have taken the liberty of writing to you directly.

Thus far, I have never once held any official position, no matter what house I stayed with. By now I am advanced in age and on top of that I am of late suffering from poor health so that, as far as my social position is concerned, I have no ambitions whatsoever. Were I to come and stay with you, I would be content with a suit of armor and a spare horse in case, at some stage, I would have to go into battle. I have no wife or children, and since I am an old man I would be content with whatever house and furniture you would provide.

From a young age I have, in all, gone into battle some six times, four times out of which I was in the absolute vanguard. This is widely known, and of course there is also proof of it. However, it is not at all with a view to advance my social position that I mention this.

I could be of use in matters concerning the use of weapons and the battlefield, and in the event, on how to subdue a province.

I have dedicated myself to these matter from my early youth, disciplining myself over many years, so that, if it were required, I would put myself at your service.

Yours Sincerely,

In the second month of the seventeenth year of Kanei [April 1640]

Miyamoto Musashi

Lord Tadatoshi hired Musashi on a stipend sufficient to support seventeen servants, and also gave him three hundred *koku* in kind. Perhaps it was because Musashi stayed in his lordship's domain as a guest that he was not taken up in his retinue of retainers, and that his dwelling was situated at a high place such as Kumamoto's Chiba castle.

• It is indicative of the author's limited knowledge about Musashi's early life that already, less than a third into his narrative, Masanaga has reached the point where Musashi settles in Kumamoto. This contrasts sharply with Tanji Hōkin, who is already two-thirds into writing his *Bushū denraiki* before he has reached the same point—which, conversely, illustrates Hōkin's limited knowledge of Musashi's later life.

- Iwama Rokubei Masanari is believed to have been the oldest son of Takeda Yoshinobu, a descendant of none other than the famous Takeda Shingen (1521–73). Masanari had first been in the service of Ogasawara Hidemasa (1569–1615), the father of Musashi's former host, Tadazane. In 1609, however, he entered the service of the Hosokawa, when he was made to accompany Hidemasa's second daughter upon her marriage into the Hosokawa clan. Given Masanari's former service to the Ogasawara, it is clear why he would have been chosen to approach Musashi, who was then still living on the estate of Hidemasa's son, Tadazane.

- Sakazaki Naizen was a descendant of the Okada, a clan distantly related to the *Bukōden*'s author. Naizen's adoptive ancestors hailed from the province of Owari where they had served Oda Nobunaga's father, Oda Nobuhide (1510–51). They, too, at some stage entered the service of the Ogasawara, but later settled as cattle farmers in the vicinity of Kumamoto, where they entered the service of the Hosokawa. It was not long after that Naizen was adopted by Sakazaki Kiyosaemon, who by then had risen to the position of junior head of pages on a stipend of close to two thousand *koku*. By the time Musashi wrote his letter, Naizen had succeeded his father as junior head of pages on a stipend of one thousand *koku*.

- The *Bukōden* is one of the few records to mention where exactly Musashi lived after he had settled in Kumamoto. Somewhat confusingly, the place Masanaga describes as Chiba castle was situated within the walls of Kumamoto castle. Situated inside one of the curves of the Hirai river, on the northwestern side of the castle grounds, it was the original site of Kumamoto castle. It is not clear why the place was called Chiba castle, as the former castle, too, was know by the name of Kumamoto, albeit written with different characters. Today, the area is still known as the Chiba castle district, or Chibajō *machi*, although it is now situated outside the castle grounds.

❧ Musashi's Daily Life in Higo

At Kumamoto, Musashi led a peaceful and quiet life and frequently visited Akiyama Wanao, the chief abbot of the Taishō temple and passed the days in composing *renga*, practicing calligraphy, and making handicrafts. As a result, there are a great number of sword sheaths, bows, *bokutō*, *renga*, and calligraphies from his hand.

According to the *Dosui dengen*, the *deshi* who assembled under Musashi in Higo included, beginning with Lord Hosokawa Tadatoshi, among others, Nagaoka Shikibe Yoriyuki, Sawamura Usaemon Tomoyoshi, and a host of other Hosokawa retainers, both favored and not favored, as well as foot soldiers and administrators, some thousand men in all.

The brothers Terao Magonojo [Nobumasa] and Terao Motomenosuke Nobuyuki were on intimate terms with Musashi and would often work with him on tactics, without joining the other *deshi* in practice. Eventually, the two brothers became the sole progenitors of the Niten Ichi school of swordsmanship.

Musashi's execution of the art of *heihō* was exceedingly quiet, as if one were watching a Noh performance. (According to Nakanishi Magonojō, usually, Musashi would not resort to the art of *heihō*).

- Akiyama Wanao (1618–73), was the second abbot of the Taishō temple, built in 1637 to serve as the Hosokawa family temple in Kumamoto.
- Dosui was the Buddhist name of Yamamoto Gengosaemon Katsuyasu, a retainer of the Nagaoka Okinaga who had followed the Hosokawa to Higō and was now the keeper of Yatsushiro castle, some twenty miles south along the coast from Kumamoto. In retirement Katsuyasu had recorded his memoirs in a work called the *Dosui dengen* (*The Dosui Transmissions*), although it is possible that Masanaga is merely referring to (the title of) a passage in his father's records concerning Katsuyasu.
- Sawamura Usaemon Tomoyoshi (1605–65) was a senior retainer of the Hosokawa and became a close friend of Musashi during his years in Higo.
- Terao Magonojō Nobumasa (1611–72) was a retainer of Hosokawa Tadatoshi and lived near his lord's headquarters of Kumamoto castle. Like Musashi, Nobumasa never accepted any official post, dedicating his life instead to mastering Musashi's Niten Ichi-ryū. In this he succeeded when, along with his brother, Terao Motomenosuke Nobuyuki, he became one of the three men selected by Musashi to keep his school of swordsmanship alive. It was to Nobumasa that Musashi dedicated and entrusted his *Book of Five rings*. Nobumasa passed Musashi's teachings on to Shibatō Yoshinori, who in turn passed it on to, Yoshida Sanetsura (teacher of the author of the *Bushū denraiki*, Tanji Hōkin). To Nobuyuki, however, Musashi passed on his *Heihō sanjū-kyū kajō*, the *Thirty-nine Articles on the Art of Heihō* in which Musashi had first sought to organize his thoughts on the Niten Ichi school of swordsmanship.
- Nakanishi Magonojō Munemasa (1604–1700) was, like Yamamoto Katsuyasu, a retainer of the Nagaoka clan. He was a descendant of the Akashi, a clan that hailed from

the same province as Musashi and like him related to the Akamatsu. Though Munemasa served the Nagaoka in the capacity of Magistrate of Wardrobes, he played an active part in the suppression of the Shimabara Rebellion, receiving praise for his display of valor and an increase of his stipend to 130 *koku*. It is believed that Munemasa, too, was among Musashi's many *deshi* and according to Masanaga he looked after Musashi in old age.

❷ Shimizu Hōki's Query

One year, on the third of January, during an evening ceremony to celebrate the new year, all the elders, senior retainers, and *bushi* were seated according to their rank, and among them was Musashi.

At one point, before the ceremony had yet started, and those in attendance were talking among themselves, master Shimizu Hōki leant over to Musashi and said: "It is rumored that when you fought Yoshioka Seijūrō [Naoshige] some years ago, it was he who dealt the first blow. Is it true?"

Without replying, Musashi suddenly stood up and sat down next to master Hōki with a candle holder, saying: "When I was young I suffered from scabies on my head, and since it would be a poor sight if I shaved the top of my head, I grew my hair long. During the duel with Sejūrō, he was fighting with a real sword, while I was fighting with a *bokutō*. Now wouldn't you say that when one is struck by a real sword there should be a scar? So please take a close look." And saying this, he parted his hair with his right hand and held the candle up to his head with his left hand in front of master Hōki's face.

Backing away, Hōki replied: "No, I cannot see any scars." But Musashi insisted, saying: "Please take a really close look." And Hōki did so, saying: "You are right, I have looked close-ly." At this Musashi immediately stood up again and, putting the candle holder back, returned to his seat, where he stroked down his hair and sat down with utter composure. During the exchange, the gathered samurai had held their breath, clenching their fists, their palms wet with perspiration.

It seems that from that time onward the people of Kumamoto believed that master Hōki had made the blunder of his life. It was an example of Musashi's bold spirit.

- Shimizu Hōki (1573–1649) was a famous warrior in the island of Kyushu. He had won fame during the second Korean campaign, when he had fought under the great Katō Kiyomasa. In 1602 he had entered the service of Hosokawa Tadaoki on a stipend of two thousand *koku*. By the time Musashi came to Higo, Hōki had climbed to the lofty position of senior scribe on a stipend of close to five thousand *koku*. It seems that Hōki was a keen practition-er of the Yagyū Shinkage-ryū, which may account for Musashi's snub.

❷ The Bout With his Friend Shiota Hamanosuke

Shiota Hamanosuke, an expert in the art of *hoshu jutsu*, was a retainer of Lord Hosokawa Tadaoki with five men under his command and a stipend of fifteen *koku*. Eager to test his skills he challenged the swordsman to a bout and, of course, Musashi willingly complied. But Hamanosuke was utterly unable to touch

Musashi with his *bokutō*. And when he resorted to his *hoshu jutsu*, Musashi simply sat down, telling him that he would floor him if he came within reach. This greatly angered Hamanosuke, who tried a technique on Musashi, but he was unable to come within reach of the swordsman without getting the worst of it. At this Hamanosuke expressed his admiration and it was from then on that he became one of Musashi's *deshi*.

Given that Hamanosuke was adept at the art of *hoshu jutsu*, he also taught its techniques to Musashi's other *deshi*, except Terao Motomenosuke's son, Kintabei, who was strongly built, and was chosen to be taught in the art of swordsmanship by his father. It was because of Shiota Hamanosuke that some of the *hoshu jutsu* techniques have found their way into the Niten Ichi school of swordsmanship.

• Not much is known about Shiota Hamanosuke. Like Musashi, he was born in the province of Harima, where he grew up in the village of Shiota, the place from which his family derived its name. It was there that he entered the service of Hosokawa Tadaoki, at that time still the master of Miyazu castle in the neighboring province of Tango. Whilst in Tadaoki's service he became an expert in the art of *hoshu jutsu*. On Tadaoki's promotion, Hamanosuke followed his lord to Kokura and it was there that he and Musashi met for the first time.

It was probably because of their shared background that, in spite of Hamanosuke's temper, he and Musashi became friends. According to the *Bushū denraiki* Musashi visited Hamanosuke at least twice, and it is likely that he was a regular guest at his house, since Musashi was a regular visitor to Kokura. Hamanosuke also followed the Hosokawa to Kumamoto, where, again according to the *Bushū denraiki*, the new lord, Hosokawa Tadatoshi, ordered him to manage Musashi's estate so that the aging swordsman need not concern himself with such matters. Shiota Hamanosuke died in 1648, three years after Musashi had passed away.

- *Hoshu jutsu* is a compendium of seizing, holding, and binding techniques employed to arrest culprits or deal with those who were captured alive during siege warfare. As such they helped to form the foundation of the modern day martial art of *jūjutsu*.

❷ The Gestation of the *Book of Five Rings*

In February of the eighteenth year of Kanei [March 1641], on the orders of Lord Tadatoshi, Musashi composed the *Heihō sanjū-kyū kajō*, a treatise on the art of *heihō*, and presented it to his lordship.

Then, on October 10 of the twentieth year of Kanei [November 21, 1643], Musashi first compiled the *Book of Five Rings* at Mount Iwato, in the province of Higo.

Musashi asked Akiyama Wanao, the second-generation abbot of the Taishō temple to correct its preface. Fearful that the text might lose its true meaning through any elaborations, Akiyama refrained from changing the structure of the text in any way, limiting himself to the correction of wrongly written characters and citing old sayings that immediately pertained to the text.

- The *Heihō sanjū-kyū kajō*, or the *Thirty-nine Articles on the Art of Heihō* were Musashi's first attempt to organize his thoughts on the Niten Ichi school of swordsmanship. As such they were to form the basis of his *Book of Five Rings*.

It is significant that Masanaga speaks of "thirty-nine articles," as opposed to thirty-five, for this is the number of articles in which this text is nowadays found (but then, of course, under the title *Heihō sanjū-go kajō*). To make matters even more confusing, there is even a version comprising forty-two articles (the *Heihō shijū-ni kajō*). It is not clear whether clauses were deleted or added by Musashi's followers, but the fact remains that today there are three versions with three different numbers of clauses in existence.

The *Nitenki*, by contrast, refers to thirty-five articles, but this might simply be due to the fact that its author was only familiar with a version comprising the corresponding number. In the absence of any evidence to the contrary, we have to assume that Masanaga is correct in his assertion, especially because he later mentions that, on June 6, 1645, while on his deathbed, Musashi handed "the thirty-nine articles" over to his *deshi* Terao Motomenosuke Nobuyuki, and not thirty-five.

❷ Musashi Falls Ill

In the summer of the second year of Shōhō [1645], Musashi fell ill. Finding the hustle and bustle of town disagreeable, he went up to Mount Iwato, where he entered the Reigan cave so that he might quietly await his end.

Strange but groundless rumors were beginning to circulate among the populace and, feigning that he had gone out to hunt with falcons, Lord Nagaoka Yoriyuki prevailed on Musashi and eventually made him return to the old residence of Chiba castle.

- Mount Iwato is situated just west of Kumamoto castle. Musashi, at this time, was living on the grounds of

Kumamoto castle, where, with the blessing of Hosokawa Tadatoshi, he had settled to spend his last days. Mount Iwato is the location of the Reigandō, the cave historically connected to the worship of the Kannon Bosatsu (Avalokitesvara), the bodhisattva of compassion. Two years earlier, Hosokawa Tadatoshi had passed away and it is believed that it was on the request of his son, Hosokawa Mitsunao (1619–50), that Musashi recorded the secrets of his school of swordsmanship.

- Nagaoka Yoriyuki (1616–66) was the son of Nagaoka Okinaga. Okinaga was by now sixty-three, an old man in medieval Japan, and it is highly likely that he was unable to travel all the way up to Mount Iwato from his castle at Yatsushiro (more than a twenty-mile ride as the crow flies), and thus sent his son instead.

  Yoriyuki, who was by now twenty-nine, played a far more active role in looking after the old swordsman than this brief passage suggests. By the time Yoriyuki persuaded the old swordsman to return to Kumamoto, he and Musashi's son, Iori, had frequently exchanged letters. Iori, who, through his father's mediation, had entered the service of the Ogasawara clan, was tied down in Kokura and it is clear from his letters that he had very much come to rely on Yoriyuki for Musashi's care—a care that caused him to write his letter of gratitude already quoted in the introduction.

- As pointed out before, the place Masanaga describes as the old residence of Chiba castle was situated within the walls of Kumamoto castle. Masanaga probably refers to Musashi's dwelling as the "old residence," because Chiba castle had once been the residence of the Ideta, an old clan from Kyushu. Chiba castle had been erected in the second half of the fifteenth century by Ideta Hidenobu, but later replaced by Kumamoto castle, albeit at a slightly different location.

Musashi's Legacy I

The Transmission of Musashi's Writings

On May 12 of the second year of Shōhō [June 6, 1645], Musashi handed the *Book of Five Rings* to Terao Magonojō Nobumasa (who afterwards took the tonsure and took on the name of Muse). The *Heihō sanjū-kyū kajō* he handed to Terao Motomenosuke Nobuyuki. That same day he drafted a scroll with injunctions. (The preface to the *Book of Five Rings*, Musashi's secret writings, the scrolls with injunctions, and the writings passed down to Mogonojō are now in the possession of the Toyoda clan.)

- It was customary for clan leaders in Musashi's day to leave a list of injunctions for posterity, the so-called *kakun*, to be handed down from generation to generation. Some of the most famous lines in this vein are from the hand of Hōjō Shigetoki (1198–1261), who left a long list of instructions to his son, Nagatoki (who had just been appointed to the important office of the shogun's deputy at Kyoto), exhorting him to "use the same kind of language and give the same kind of treatment to all, so you may get the best out of the worst." A somewhat different approach was taken by the pragmatic Asakura Takakage (1428–81), who advised his successors not to "appoint people without ability simply because they have served the Asakura for generations." Most famous among all these writings are Tokugawa Ieyasu's *Teachings on the Conduct of Life*, in which

he reminds his subjects that "a man's life is like a long journey with a heavy burden," that one "need not hurry," and
that "patience is the foundation of eternal peace."

Like those by Ieyasu, Musashi's injunctions were not
so much intended for his descendants (for he had none),
but rather for his followers, and it is a mark of their devotion that the injunctions have survived until the present
day. Two versions are still in existence, one consisting of
nineteen, the other twenty-one injunctions. Both carry the
title of *Dokkōdō*, or *The Way to be Followed Alone*. Though both
versions carry Musashi's signature it is almost certain
that at least one was drafted by one of his followers. There
is no conclusive evidence as to which of the two might be
genuine, but it is widely assumed Musashi wrote twenty-
one injunctions and that, therefore, the longer version is
probably from the master's own hand.

❷ Musashi's Mortuary Tablet

Musashi's Buddhist mortuary tablet can be seen in the Kajiya
district of Kumamoto, when one visits the Yōjū temple. Its inscription runs as follows:

Progenitor of the Heihō Niten Ichi-ryū, Shinmen Musashi
Fujiwara Genshin Niten Dōraku sensei, Died on May
19 in the second year of Shōhō [June 13, 1645]

Second Generation Heihō Niten Ichi-ryū Practitioner,
Shinmen Bennosuke Koji Genshin Nobumori sensei, July
7 in the fourteenth year of Genroku [August 28, 1701]

•Oddly, Masanaga here omits any mention of Musashi's death

and burrial and proceeds to point out the location of Musashi's Buddhist mortuary tablet (*ihai*) in the precincts of the Yōjū temple. It is not clear wether this is a mistake or intentional, although the author amply makes up for this initial lacuna during the writing of the second scroll, in which he dedicates several paragraphs to the circumstances surrounding Musashi's death.

- The Yōjū temple stood just south of Kumamoto castle, on the northern bank of the Shira river. Though the temple has long since gone, a stone version of Musashi's mortuary tablet survived right up until the Second World War, when it was sadly destroyed by fire as a result of allied bombings. At that time it stood on the grounds of the Taigan temple, half a mile further north along the riverbank, at the site of what had once been the home of Akiyama Wanao's Taishō temple.

- Shinmen Bennosuke Nobumori (1666–1701) was not, as the name suggests, a relative of Musashi, but Terao Nobuyuki's fourth son. Nobumori, who would undoubtedly have been a practitioner of the Niten Ichi-ryū, died at the young age of thirty-five. Motomenosuke had named the boy after Musashi, and it was probably both in honor of his teacher and to remember his son that he inscribed Nobumori's name on Musashi's tombstone.

☯ Hayashi Razan's Tribute to Musashi

Among Musashi's many *deshi* a trusted vassal by the name of Ishikawa Sakyō painted an image of Musashi and, through the mediation of Itasaka Bokusai, approached Hayashi Razan to write a tribute to the swordsman.

That tribute is recorded in the *Hayashi Razan bunshū* and reads as follows:

Tribute to Shinmen Genshin

"Hitting the whirlwind, hitting the row of racks," they are the falsehoods of Puhua. The green snake that leaps out of the inner sleeve, it is the magic of the mountain wizard. The swordsman Shinmen Genshin carries a sword in each hand and calls his school of swordsmanship the Nittō Ichi-ryū. Whether striking or stabbing, the modulation between right and left, the elasticity of right and wrong, are born in the mind and communicated to the hands, so that the strike becomes a crushing blow, the attack a crushing defeat, and one is bound to say that "one sword cannot beat two." These are anything but the falsehoods of Puhua, the magic of the mountain wizard. How desirable it would be to have ten thousand of one's enemies study this art of *heihō*. For it is evocative of the long sword of the Marquis of Huaiyang, and with it the Chinese emperor would lose neither his right- nor his left-hand general. Truly, is such an art of *heihō* not worthy of being compared to the Chinese proverb that teaches us how one can conquer huge armies with small means?

Hayashi Razan

- Itasaka Bokusai (1578–1655) was a physician in the service of Tokugawa Ieyasu and a close friend of Hayashi Razan. He lived in the Edo's Asakusa district, where, in 1644, he opened Japan's first public library.
- Hayashi Razan (1583–1657) was a Neo-Confucian schol-

ar who served as tutor the first four shoguns of the Tokugawa Bakufu. Razan was a man of demonic energy who almost single-handedly established Neo-Confucianism as the official Bakufu creed. He wrote countless scholarly works which were posthumously compiled into the *Hayashi Razan bunshū* (*The Collected Works of Hayashi Razan*) and the *Razan sensei isshū* (*Master Razan's Poems*) by his third son Hayashi Gahō. During his life, Razan compiled a vast library on the premise of his Edo residence, which he converted into a Confucian college called Kokunkan. It was Yamaga Sokō (1622–1685), incidentally, a student of that college who took the first steps to codify the ethics of Bushidō.

- Puhua (?–860), or Fuke, in Japanese, was a Chinese monk at the time of the Tang dynasty and a student of the famous Linji Yixuan (800–66), founder of the Linji (Rinzai) School of Chan (Zen) Buddhism. Puhua is believed to have walked the streets carrying a large wind bell and chanting the kind of incantations Razan here quotes. Puhua's strand of Buddhism was introduced to Japan sometime during the thirteenth century, where it became known as Fuke Zen.

- The Marquis of Huaiyang, Han Xin (?–196 BC) was a Chinese martial strategist who is believed to have studied the art of swordsmanship from his early youth. His military genius led him to become a great military commander in the forces of Gaozu (256–195 BC), the first emperor of the Han Dynasty, and the same emperor to which Razan is referring.

Both Marquis Han Xin and Emperor Gaozu feature prominently in the *Shiji*, the *Records of the Grand Historian*, one of the first systematical overviews of more than two thousand years of Chinese history, which was written between 109 and 91 BC by the famous Chinese historian Sima Qian (145–86 BC).

The episode to which Razan refers concerns a critical stage in Gaozu's struggle against Qin dominance. It recounts how Han Xin, who at this point was in charge of the emperor's food stores, decided to desert during a lull in the fighting. The marquis was quickly followed by one of the emperor's most trusted generals, who nevertheless returned within two days. Asked by the emperor to explain his conduct, the general insisted that he did not desert but had simply gone in pursuit of the marquis, whom he had found and brought back. Surprised, the emperor asked why he did not go in pursuit of his other generals, would that not have been a worthier cause? To this the general replied that the marquis's strategic genius was invaluable, and that to lose both the marquis and himself would be tantamount to the emperor losing both his hands, i.e., his left- and his right-hand generals. Impressed by this argument, the emperor decided to promote the marquis to commander-in-chief of his forces.

❷ The Kokura Monument Epitaph

Musashi's monument epitaph can be seen at the castle town of Kokura in Buzen. It was composed by Akiyama Wanao, and reads as follows:

Looking up at the Heavens the True and Perfect Art of Heihō is Eternal, Even in Death.

Heihōsha Without Equal under the Heavens

Epitaph of Shinmen Musashi Genshin, last descendant of the Akamatsu of Harima.

Died at Kumamoto in the province of Higo on May 19 in the second year of Shōhō [June, 13, 1645].

Erected with respect on April 19, in the third year of Shōō [June 4, 1654] by his pious son.

"Look for the chances and respond to the changes," this is the way of the accomplished general. The practice of the martial arts and the study of soldiery are the preoccupation of an army. Who was it that let his heart play at the gate of *bun* and *bu*, that let his hands work on the practice grounds of the martial arts, and gained fame for his courage in doing so? It was the nobly born Musashi Shingen, scion of the Shinmen, last descendants of the Akamatsu of Harima, the man whose Buddhist name is Niten. By nature he had a magnanimity of heart that did not care about trifles. Truly, was this not the man called Musashi Shingen?

He became the progenitor of the Niten art of *heihō*. The Buddhist name of his father, Shinmen, who came from a house known for its mastery of the *jitte*, was Muni. This tradition was passed on to Musashi, who, as a result of training from dusk till dawn, came to understand that the *jitte* was many times more efficient than a single sword. However, the *jitte* was not a conventional weapon, whereas it was normal for samurai to wear two swords. And since there was no harm in applying the principles of the *jitte* to the art of fighting with two swords, he chose to abandon the tradition of fighting with the *jitte* and founded one in which one fought with two swords.

Musashi was a truly great swordsman. Whether he wielded a *shinken* or a *bokutō*, none could escape him, either by ducking or by running away. The force of his thrust resembled an arrow from a crossbow, and even the great Yōyū would not have been able to surpass him.

Musashi was a consumate master of the art of *heihō*, the embodyment of valor. Thus, at the age of thirteen, he challenged to a duel a man by the name of Arima Kihei, a Shintō-ryū swordsman from Harima, and defeated him instantly. Then, in the summer of his sixteenth year, he went to the province of Tajima. There, he challenged another swordsman and struck him dead in the blink of an eye, so that before long his name was known throughout town.

Afterwards, Musashi went up to Kyoto, where lived the Yoshioka, know as The Foremost *Heihōsha* in Japan. Musashi challenged them, and fought for his honor with a Yoshioka descendant by the name of Seijūrō on the grounds of the Rendai temple outside the capital. It was supposed to be a real contest but Musashi floored Seijūrō with a single blow of his *bokutō*, causing the latter to pass out. And because it was agreed beforehand that they would only exchange a single blow Musashi did not take Seijūrō's life. The latter's *deshi* came to his aid, lifted him on a stretcher, and took him home. There, he was given various medical treatments and eventually recovered. In the end, he abandoned the martial life and took the tonsure.

However, Yoshioka Denshichirō, too, left Kyoto to fight it out with Musashi. He attacked Musashi with a five-foot-long *bokutō*. Seizing the opportunity, Musashi wrested the *bokutō* from him and struck him with his own weapon, so that Denshichirō fell to the ground and expired.

The followers of the Yoshioka school were filled with bitterness, conspiring among themselves saying "We cannot stand up to him with technical skill alone. Let us therefore resort to tactics." And thus, feigning that they had come to practice, Yoshioka Matashichirō and his *deshi* awaited Musashi in ambush outside Kyoto at Kudarimatsu. There were several hundreds of *deshi*, intending to kill Musashi in a single attack with weapons, as well as bows and arrows. Musashi, however, had a talent for anticipating such events and, seeing through their dishonest scheme, he secretly said to his *deshi*: "This is no affair of yours, quickly leave this place. Even if my sworn enemies had assembled an army, to me it would be no more than a drifting cloud, so why should I fear them?" And when Musashi proceeded to scatter his enemies apart it seemed as if a wild dog was chasing away wild beasts. When Musashi returned to the capital having displayed his powers all its citizens were in awe. His gallant vigor, his superior calculation, the singlehanded defeat of a vast force, these were the marvelous exploits of a man of war.

Now, prior to this, successive generations of the Yoshioka clan had served as fencing instructors to the shogun. They were called "The Foremost *Heihōsha* in Japan." In the time of Shogun Yoshiaki Musashi's father, Shinmen Munisai, was summoned to the capital and ordered to duel with the Yoshioka. Of the three bouts the Yoshioka swordsman won once, while Munisai won twice. In reward for this he received the title of "*Heihōsha* Without Equal in Japan." As a result of Musashi's arrival in Kyoto and the subsequent succesive defeats of the Yoshioka swordsmen, the Yoshioka school of swordsmanship ceased to exist.

Now, near here there lived a master swordsman whose name was Ganryū. When Musashi made it known that he wanted to duel with Ganryū the latter proposed that they fight with real swords. But Musashi responded saying: "Feel free to use a real sword and display your skills with it, but I will fight with the *bokutō* and reveal its secrets." And thus both men solemnly pledged in writing that they would meet in duel on Funashima, an island in the sea between the provinces of Buzen and Nagato. And it was there that both men met at the same time. Ganryū came charging toward Musashi wielding his three-foot longsword, executing all the techniques he had to his disposal. But Musashi struck him dead with one single blow of his *bokutō*, and with a speed that seemed faster than lightning. Since Ganryū died on this island the people henceforth referred to it as Ganryū island.

From his thirteenth year until the prime of his life Musashi fought more than sixty duels without ever being beaten. He would invariably say that "In order to seize victory, one has to strike one's opponent the very moment they raise their eyebrows in surprise." And each time he met with someone in duel he lived up to this dictum. From of old thousands, nay tens of thousands have met in duel. However, except for Musashi, I have never heard of anyone to squarely face a great swordsmen and strike him dead, be it in the present or the past, in the capital or in the countryside. By now Musashi's reputation has spread throughout the country and such is the extent of his undiminished fame that it is impressed on the minds of present-day people though the oral traditions of their elders. Truly, is it not a marvel, is it not a mystery? Indeed, the excellence of his precocious talent is unparalleled.

Musashi would often say that the art of *heihō* should mature in one's hands and govern one's heart, and that as long as one remains utterly unselfish and impartial one can command armies in the field and that even the affairs of state need not be difficult. Musashi's valor at the time of the rebellion started by Lord Ishida Mitsunari, the favorite of Taikō Toyotomi Hideyoshi, or at the time of the disturbance caused by Lord Toyotomi Hideyori, cannot be expressed in words, had oceans mouths or valleys tongues, and thus I will remain silent on the matter.

Not only was Musashi a consummate swordsman, he was also at home in etiquette, music, archery, horsemanship, calligraphy, arithmetic, and poetry. Be it in his dabbling in the arts or his skillful pursuit of his profession, he was never idle. He was the model of a fine human being.

Musashi died in the province of Higo. On his deathbed he wrote the words: "Looking up at the heavens the true and perfect art of *heihō* is eternal, even in death." It was these words that have inspired me to commemorate his legacy. Hence, I, his pious son, have founded this monument, so that his words and deeds may be passed on and seen by successive generations into eternity.

- *Bun* and *bu* refers to one's civil and martial accomplishments.
- As the author points out, the *Kokura hibun*, which can still be found on the monument Miyamoto Iori erected for his adoptive father near Kokura, was written by Akiyama Wanao (1618–73), abbot of the Taishō temple in Kumamoto. During Musashi's last years in Kumamoto, Wanao had befriended the swordsman and, according to the *Bukōden*, helped him by proofreading his *Book of Five Rings*. At Musashi's deathbed he gave the swordsman his last rites and his posthumous name. In 1654, ten years after Musashi's death, Wanao is believed to have composed the lengthy epitaph on Iori's request.
- Oddly, by stating that both swordsmen "met at the same time," Wanao seems to suggest that both swordsmen arrived at Funashima island at the same moment. Both the *Bukōden* and the *Bushū denraiki* claim that the men arrived at different times, although they fail to agree on who arrived first.
- It is typical, too, that Wanao has nothing to say about his hero's activities at the time of the Battle of Sekigahara and the sieges of Osaka castle, fourteen years later. It is perhaps rather due to his poor knowledge of Musashi's early life rather than his lack of words that the abbot wisely chooses to remain silent on the issue.

❷ The Origins of the Kokura Monument Epitaph

In the spring of the seventeenth year of Kanei [1640], when he was fifty-seven, Musashi came to Higo in response to a request from Lord Hosokawa Tadatoshi. Anticipating his demise, he erected a tombstone on a hill overlooking Kokura castle, and made his way to Higo.

It was ten years later, on April 19 of the third year of Shō-ō [June 4, 1654], that Miyamoto Iori erected the Monument Epitaph, which was composed by Akiyama Wanao, abbot of the Taishō temple in Higo.

- Though Masanaga claims that Musashi came to Higo in the spring of 1640, recently uncovered documents suggest that Musashi might have arrived in Higo in the autumn of that year.
- Hosokawa Tadatoshi (1586–1641) had come a long way by the time he approached Iwama Rokubei Masanari, the keeper of his castle in Kumamoto, to see wether Musashi was willing to move to Higo. At the time of Musashi's duel with Sasaki Kojirō, he had still been lord of Moji castle, a small castle, situated at the tip of the Kiku peninsula, a few miles northeast of his father's castle at Kokura. As the third son of Hosokawa Tadaoki he had been bound to remain a minor figure in the larger feudal scheme of things. But when, in the wake of the Battle of Sekigahara, his eldest brother was disinherited, it was Tadatoshi, and not his second eldest brother (who would later join Toyotomi Hideyori at Osaka castle out of resentment), who was chosen to succeed his father and become master of Kokura castle and the clan's fiefdom in Buzen.

  Unprepared though he was for this sudden turn of events, Tadatoshi acquitted himself well — so well that in 1632 he was promoted to the Kumamoto fiefdom, a vast estate of more than five-hundred-thousand *koku* in Higo province.

The *Bukōden*
second scroll

Musashi as a Man

◉ The Adoption of Miyamoto Iori

Miyamoto Iori was born in the village of Shōhōji in the province of Dewa. His father had been a farmer, but had abandoned this life and was reduced to a life of vagrancy. They were [currently] living on a wild plot of land in the shadow of the mountains, some six miles from Shōhōji. There they had built a small thatched hut and were eking out a living by trying to cultivate the arid land, turning it into vegetable plots to stave off the day's hunger. There had been two children, a son and a daughter, but the latter had been married off to a man from the village, and since his wife had passed away, father and son were living alone in the small hut.

Now in the prime of his life, while on one of his *musha shugyō*, Musashi was traveling from province to province. At this time, the young boy was thirteen years old, precocious and good-looking. He was catching loaches in a wet paddy field beside the road along which Musashi was passing. Going up to the boy, Musashi asked him whether he would share his catch with him. The young boy said he would and, putting his catch into a small pail, handed them all to Musashi. At this Musashi said: "I am grateful for your kindheartedness, but I don't need this much, a few will suffice." And saying this, he scooped a few loaches out of the pail, wrapped them in a towel, and handed the pail back to the boy. The boy laughed and said: "It is not often that travelers ask me for loaches, so why should I be mean? Please, take the whole pail." And leaving the pail in Musashi's hands he ran off without even looking round. Delighted, Musashi accepted the gift and was filled with gratitude.

Later, while passing through the plains around the village of Shōhōji, Musashi lost his way and was unable to find a place to stay for the night. It was already getting dark, and he would have to travel seven miles as the crow flies and almost double that if he retraced his way to reach a hostel in the village. While he was wandering what to do, Musashi spotted the light of a fire in the shade of the distant mountains. Taking this as a good omen, he set off in the direction of the fire, and came upon a small thatched hut.

When Musashi knocked on the door, a young boy of thirteen or fourteen came out and asked him who he was. Musashi said: "I am a traveler unable to find lodgings without a guide and unable to go on as it has grown dark." The boy replied: As you can see, this is just an ugly old hut, just wide enough for me to live in, I fear I really cannot put you up for the night." But Musashi persisted, saying: "As I'm only traveling, any place will do. Please let me stay under your roof." The boy looked closely at Musashi and suddenly asked: "Are you not that person who asked me for some loaches the other day?" Surprised, Musashi said: "Indeed, I am that person." "In that case," the boy replied, "please come and stay under our roof," and he led Musashi inside.

When he had sat down and rested Musashi asked the boy: "Why is it that you live here by yourself at such a young age?"

The boy replied: "My mother has long since passed away and my only sister has been married off to a farmer who lives seven miles from here. I lived here together with my father, but he too has now passed away, so that I am now living here by myself." And saying this he served Musashi with a dish of millet, wished him good night and withdrew to one of the recesses of the hut. Then Musashi, too, turned in for the night, even though he somehow did not feel fully at ease.

That night Musashi was roused from his pillow by the sound of a blade being sharpened. Hearing this he thought: "Well, well, this boy seems to be the only one left from a gang of robbers, what a knave! It appears he intended to wait until I was sound asleep and kill me." but when he incidentally yawned, the mountain boy asked: "Why can't you sleep?" Musashi answered: "Hearing that sound grates on my ears. It sounds creepy, so I cannot sleep." At this the boy laughed and said: "That doesn't sound like the strong man you seem, aren't you a bit of a coward? Even if I wanted to kill you, how could I do so with these slender wrists? And why should I kill my guest?" "Then why are you sharpening that blade," asked Musashi. And while he was tidying up the hut the boy answered: "It was only yesterday that my father passed away. I wanted to bury his remains in the mountains behind the hut, next to those of my mother, but there was no one to help me, and I am to weak to carry my father's body into the mountains by myself. I though and thought about it, but since I can only carry a small load at a time, I at length decided to cut his body in half, so I could carry and bury it in turn."

Hearing this, Musashi realized how dreadful this must be and was deeply moved by the boy's resolve. He praised the boy and said: "Luckily I am staying at your home tonight. I will help you as best I can. Surely, you must be very downcast." Then, lifting the corpse by the shoulders and making the boy carry the legs, Musashi helped the boy carry the body into the mountains behind the hut. There, they dug a hole next to the boy's dead mother, buried his father and, piling stones onto the grave mound, made them serve as an epitaph. By the time they returned to the boy's dwelling it was already getting light.

The boy politely said: "It is lonely now that I am on my own. Could you not stay here and cheer me up in your spare moments?" Musashi took pity on the boy, and having reflected for a while, he said: "What good is there in you staying here by yourself? If you come with me, I might at some stage be able to help you find suitable employment." The boy said: "I see. I would indeed like to follow you, where ever it be, but I do not want to be a manservant for the rest of my life. However, if I can become a *bushi*, sitting astride a horse and carrying a lance, I would be content. If not, I would much prefer to go on living here, where I can spend my life in freedom." But Musashi said: "If you come with me, I will make sure that you become the *bushi* with his own horse and lance you so desire." The boy's face lit up as he nodded and said: "In that case, let's go together!" And he proceeded to gather his belongings in preparation for the journey.

Seeing this, Musashi said: "Does your coming with me not cause any problems for anybody else?" But the boy said: "My only sister lives in the village of Shōhōji, but for a long time now I haven't heard from her." Apart from her, I have no one, so there is no need for any leave-taking. This thatched hut, too, was just built by me and my father, and there is no need to leave it behind." And having said this, he set fire to the hut and let it burn to the ground. Then he prepared himself for the journey ahead and, tucking his knife under his belt, set out in Musashi's footsteps.

From then on the two of them traveled through various provinces, during the course of which the youngster became adept in the art of *heihō*. He was given the name of Miyamoto Iori and entered the service of the house of Ogasawara in the province of Buzen on a stipend of two thousand *koku*. At length, he reached the rank of those with their own horse and *yari*, as he had originally wished, and his descendants, too, continued to serve as retainers at the castle of Kokura.

- Though a fascinating read, this account of Musashi's adoption is at least partly fictional. From the family records of the Miyamoto clan in Kokura, as well as a *munafuda* (a sign staked to a traditional building stating the building's donor, builder, and date of construction) recently uncovered from the Tomari shrine of Yoneda village, it is now clear that Iori was a native of Harima, where he was born as the second son of a certain Tawara Hisamitsu, a samurai in the service of Bessho Nagaharu (1558–80), the lord of Miki castle. Hisamitsu's lord had initially supported Nobunaga's drive westward, but due to his wife's clan relations, he stubbornly refused to submit to the rule of Toyotomi Hideyoshi, at that time Nobunaga's chief general in the region. Banding up with the other Besshō chieftains he began to attack Hideyoshi's forces, even calling in the help of the powerful Mōri. His resistance proved so fierce, that at one stage, Hideyoshi's army was forced to retreat, which so enraged the great general that he laid siege to Miki castle. Finally, in January 1580, having held out for a year and ten months, the members of the Bessho clan agreed to commit *seppuku* on the condition that those who had served them would be spared. Reduced to the life of a *rōnin*, Tawara Hisamitsu took up farming near Yoneda, where he had two sons, the second of whom was Iori.

This version of events is largely confirmed by the *Harima kagami*, a topography compiled in 1762 by Hirano Yōsai, who claims that Iori "was born in the village of Yoneda. His father, who was called Jinbei, was formerly a samurai at Miki castle of the Bessho clan, but following the fall of the castle, he moved to the village of Yoneda, where he sired Iori." It goes on to explain that "One day, the house of Ogasawara, masters of Akashi castle, invited Miyamoto Musashi, the swordsman without equal, to come and stay with them as their guest. Iori, who at this time was sixteen years old, was in the service of the Ogasawara, and Musashi was so impressed with the boy's charm, that he adopted him."

Masanaga's claim, then, that Musashi encountered Iori while passing through the village of Shōhōji seems farfetched, but this is not necessarily so. There used to be another village that went by the name of Shōhōji, and that village was situated in the province of Harima. Significantly, while it corresponds in pronunciation, the northern village is written with different characters than those written down by Masanaga, whereas the village in Harima is written with exactly the same characters, although it has by now disappeared from Japanese maps. This village was situated some ten miles north of Akashi castle, in the Miki district of Harima province. Though it is still called Shōhōji, today, it is part of the Bessho district of Miki city.

❧ Iori's Perspicacity

One day, Miyamoto Iori had departed from Kokura castle in a palanquin and was being carried along a narrow road, when on a nearby military exercise field he saw what seemed to be a traveling medicine salesman, pacing around the field. A manservant in front of him was carrying a bag of gold brocade, while the salesman loudly proclaimed that it contained the cure of all one's ailments. Seeing the spectacle from his palanquin, Iori's interest was raised and, calling one of his pages, he said: "Find out where that person is from, put him up in the first good hostel and tell him in no uncertain terms to return whence he has come." When the page had conveyed the message, it proved that the men were from Osaka and the next day they were sent away by boat.

It was one year later that Yuishō Masayuki and Maruhashi Chūya were sentenced to death at Fuchū in the province of Suruga. Judging by their appearance it seemed that Masayuki was the very same person as the former medicine salesman. Asked how he had known that it was Masayuki when he expelled the medicine salesman, Iori answered, "I never knew it was Masayuki. Nor did I inquire into his age or see his face." Hearing this, his peers again asked: "Then why was it that you expelled him when you met him on the exercise grounds?" And Iori said: "It was just that his appearance wasn't normal. He seemed to be measur-

ing up the field in paces. At this, I grew suspicious, so I evict-
ed him from my lord's fief without further ado." This was
truly an example of Iori's great insight.

As can be read in the historical records, the incident with Yuishō
Masayuki and Maruhashi Chūya took place in July in the
fourth year of Keian [August 1651]. The account of Iori's
exceptional talents was given by Muraya Kanpachirō.

- The incident to which Masanagi is referring here has gone
  down in Japanese history as the Keian Disturbance (Keian
  no hen). Shortly after the death of the third Tokugawa shōgun, Iemitsu (1604–51), a number of *rōnin*, led by the
  Hōzōin-ryū adept Maruhashi Chūya and the *heihōsha* Yuishō
  Masayuki, conspired to topple the Bakufu. The plot, however, was uncovered and all its participants put to death.
- Muraya Kanpachirō here is the same merchant from Kokura
  on whose account Masanaga's father based his account
  of the duel on Ganryū island.

❧ The *Renga* Meetings

Lord Nagaoka Yoriyuki now was a great lover of *renga* and,
in one of the *yashiki* in the second ring of Kumamoto castle, he
would often organize meetings to composed *renga*. These meetings would be attended by Nagaoka Umanusuke Shigemasa,
Musashi, and Morisaki Gensan, as well as a number of other
renga lovers. No sooner would they begin than they would all
join in, composing poems as they went along, but all who attended remarked to each other that throughout the meetings Musashi
did not compose one line.

Whenever Musashi came to the *yashiki* of Nagaoka Yoriyuki at the castle's second ring, Yamamoto Gengosaemon [Katsuyasu], followed by all his *deshi*, would come out into the entrance to welcome Musashi.

One day, as he entered the house, Musashi uttered a cry and had to hold on to the wooden paneling to lift himself onto the raised floor at the entrance. Genosaemon went up to him and asked him if he needed a hand, but Musashi put him at ease and said he was fine.

From this it can be seen that the retainers of the house of Nagaoka regarded Musashi with the same reverence as their own military commanders.

- A *renga*, or linked verse poem, is a series of short verses that are linked into one single poem through a collaborative effort. The *renga* is usually opened with a reference to the season in which the meeting is held and should have touched on all seasons when complete. The principal rules in *renga* are link and shift, meaning that each new verse should connect to the previous verse but that it should also move on by drawing on new imagery.
- Nagaoka Umanusuke Shigemasa was not a descendant of the Nagaoka clan but a cousin of Hosokawa Tadaoki.
- Morisaki Gensan was a highly cultured physician and tea master who had entered the service of Hosokawa Tadatoshi in 1637 and continued to serve the Hosokawa until his death in 1655.
- Yamamoto Gengosaemon Katsuyasu was a retainer of the Nagaoka and the keeper of Yatsushiro castle. In retirement Katsuyasu took on the name of Dosui and recorded his memoirs in a work called the *Dosui dengen* (*The Dosui*

Transmissions). It is probably from the *Dosui dengen* that Masanaga drew his account of the *renga* meetings.

❧ Musashi During the Great Fire

One day there was a fire in Kumamoto's Shinchō district, when a man was seen, crossing a ladder he had laid across the roofs of the houses that stood shoulder to shoulder in the district's cramped quarters. Seeing this the people were taken aback and inquired who it was, but no one seemed to know and all they could do was stand back in awe. It was only afterward that it transpired that the man in question had been Musashi. Now on normal days Musashi's demeanor would be far from lively but rather serene, so that he looked exceedingly old, indeed, so old that Gengosaemon had felt obliged to help him enter Lord Nagaoka's *yashiki*. In truth, however, his agility and nimbleness was as described above, a quality hard to value at its true merits.

Thus it was said by Nakanishi [Magonojō Munemasa].

- The Shinchō district was — and still is — situated just south of Kumamoto castle, not far from the old site of Chiba castle where Musashi resided.
- Nakanishi Magonojō Munemasa (1604–1700) was a retainer of the Nagaoka clan. He was a descendant of the Akashi, a clan that hailed from the same province as Musashi and like him related to the Akamatsu. Though Munemasa served the Nagaoka in the capacity of Magistrate of Wardrobes, he played an active part in the Shimabara Rebellion, receiving praise for his display of valor and an increase of his stipend to 130 *koku*. Munemas, according to Masanaga, was one of Musashi's *deshi* and looked after him in old age.

❧ The Banquet

Once, Musashi held a gorgeous banquet under the blossoming cherry trees in the company of master Sawamura Usaemon [Tomoyoshi] and half of his *deshi*. All were sitting down, Musashi at the head and his pupils in two rows. The party was getting lively as master Usaemon offered a cup of sake to make a toast and one of his attendants served appetizers. Then, just as Musashi was about to take a snack with his right hand, a kite descended from the sky with the speed of lightning and sought to fly off with the delicacy. Instantly Musashi drew his *tantō* with his left hand and impaled the bird on the dagger. All who heard of the feat were astounded at the speed of his technique.

I later heard from Fukuda that the kite in question had nested among the cherry grove for many years, and that whenever spring came it had preyed on the appetizers that were served during the attending festivities. Indeed, there was not one who had attended one of these banquets who had not at one stage been the victim of the kite's gluttony. Having said that, Musashi was totally unaware of this. Moreover, to impale the kite with his left hand surely made even lightning seem slow.

- Sawamura Usaemon Tomoyoshi (1605–65) was a senior retainer of the Hosokawa and became a close friend of Musashi during his later years in Higo.

❧ Lord Yoriyuki's Query

One day Lord Yoriyuki asked Musashi how one could select the right bamboo for the rod of a banner. He had brought along several lengths of fresh bamboo his men had harvested in his domains in Tamana.

Musashi asked him to hand him a bunch and, holding them at their lower end with one hand, brandished them as one would a sword, causing several lengths to break under the strain. Carefully selecting the broken from the unbroken, he took the undamaged lengths of bamboo and, giving them to Lord Yoriyuki, said: "These will do." Exasperated, Lord Yoriyuki laughed and said: "Truly, that is a good way of selecting the right bamboo, but who on earth is able to brandish a bunch of bamboo with one hand like you?" For though Musashi was a man of exceptional strength, there were few like him.

Thus is was said by Yamamoto Dosui.

- A banner (*hatasashi* or *sashimono*) here is the Japanese equivalent of the European medieval heraldic banner. Japanese medieval banners were narrow vertical flags that identified the chieftain under whom soldiers were fighting by the latter's family crest (*kamon*) or the clan's battle slogan.

  Sashimono could be worn by footsoldiers (*ashigaru*), who attached the bamboo pole to which the banners were fastened to their backs. They could also be carried by mounted warriors, in which case the bamboo pole was inserted into a special holder attached to the saddle.

- Yamamoto Gengosaemon Katsuyasu (Dosui) was a retainer of the Nagaoka and the master of Yatsushiro castle. In retirement Katsuyasu took on the name of Dosui and recorded his memoirs in a work called the *Dosui dengen* (*The Dosui Transmissions*).

❧ Testing Musashi's Patience

Every now and then Musashi would be summoned before his lordship for a talk. It was prior to such a meeting that his lordship turned to his attendants and said that he wanted to pull a prank on Musashi and that they should think of one. They said this would be difficult but that they would try to think of a ruse. Now whenever Musashi was summoned before his lordship he would be seated in the anteroom with his hands touching the lintel in which the sliding doors ran that separated the two rooms. And thus, on the appointed day, they waited for Musashi to arrive, hoping to pincer his head between the sliding doors.

Before long Musashi arrived, placing his hands on the lintel as was his wont. He was well into his conversation with his lordship when the sliding doors were shut with a slam. Yet Musashi remained unperturbed and continued the conversation as if nothing had happened. His lordship was intrigued, but when he took a closer look he noticed that Musashi had placed his folding fan on top of the lintel, leaving a space between the two sliding doors of well over a foot wide and his head untouched. His lordship praised Musashi greatly, for it was now clear to him now that at no instant did Musashi ever let up his guard. Thus we may learn greatness by observing the small things in life.

❧ Musashi's Death and Burial

On the nineteenth of May in the second year of Shōho [July 12, 1645], Musashi passed away in his house at [the former site of] Chiba castle in Kumamoto.

Before he passed away, feeling that he was about to die, he expressed to Lord Nagaoka Yoriyuki his wish that he might be attended by someone who had shown merit during the siege of Hara castle. And thus Nakanishi Magonojō Munemasa was chosen to remain by Musashi's side during his last days.

On his death Musashi was laid in his coffin in full armor with all his weapons, as he had requested. He was buried in the village of Oe in the Akita district. As was previously arranged, the coffin was brought to the Maesugi horse grounds of the Taishō temple, where Akiyama Wanao performed the last rites. All this was done according to Musashi's will.

Afterwards, when Lord Yoriyuki went out falcon hunting, he visited Musashi's grave, and summoning the village elder, told him not to tarry in keeping the grave clean and tidy and gave him fifty bags of rice by way of payment. The next day the village elder came to Lord Yoriyuki's *yashiki* at the second ring of Kumamoto castle, where he handed in Lord Yoriyuki's promissory note and took receipt of the rice. It seems that Magonojō's son, Kakunoshin, accompanied the village elder on that occasion and had seen the promissory note with his own eyes.

- Hara castle was the castle at the center of the Shimabara Rebellion.
- Today, neither the village Oe nor the district of Akita any longer exist, as the village has been swallowed up by Kumamoto's suburbs, while the district of Akita was abolished as a result of land reforms during the Meiji era. In Musashi's day, however, the village of Oe was situated on the eastern banks of the Shira river, only a mile or so

from Kumamoto castle. Spelled with a different initial character, this part of Kumamoto is now called Ōe.

- Akiyama Wanao's Taishō temple stood on the west side of the Shira river, not far from where it curves sharply eastward, out of Kumamoto. It seems, then, that on Musashi's death at his house on the grounds of Kumamoto castle, his coffin was carried north along the western embankment of the Shira river, to the Taishō temple, where Akiyama Wanao performed the last rites for his spiritual friend. From there, the coffin was carried across the river to be buried in a cemetery in the village of Oe.

  Today, the Taishō temple is still the site of a modest memorial monument to the swordsman.

- It seems that Nakanishi Munemasa was one of Oe's inhabitants, a fact that may have played an important role in Musashi's wish to be buried there, close to those who continued the tradition of his school of swordsmanship.

Musashi's Legacy II

Musashi Armor

Musashi's saddle was made by Nakanishi Magonojō Munemasa according to the traditions of the house of Nakanishi, and bore a family crest consisting of four diamonds. It has since been destroyed by fire.

Musashi left the sword forged by Ōhara Sanemori to his friend Sawamura Usaemon [Tomoyoshi]. Even now the sword is part of the heirloom of the house of Sawamura. Its length is said to be approximately three feet. It seems that the sword was at the center of an extraordinary incident at the time of the second Sawamura generation. Since then it has never been worn but permanently kept as relic of devotion a in a box tied down with a *shimenawa*. Today there are only few who wear a three-foot longsword. The sword is exceedingly sharp and a true work of craftsmanship. This is what has been told to me by Toyoda Kennai.

On July 25, in the seventh year of Meiwa [August 14, 1770], a fire erupted in Kumamoto's Tsuboi district and spread to the Kyō district, which was reduced to ashes. The house and possessions of Sawamura Daikurō [Tomoaki] were totally destroyed by fire. Having failed to bring out the sword, Daikurō stood at the scene of the fire telling the onlookers that he did not care having lost his gold, his silver, his treasures and his possessions, but that he merely lamented having lost the *tachi* forged by Sanemori. In the event, his treasury survived the flames. It was a double-walled treasury with two padlocks, to which only members of the family had access. When, five days after the conflagration, he opened the treasury's inner door, Sanemori's sword was miraculously lying on top of the armor chest in the corner of the room. It was a miracle indeed. Come to think of it, could it be because Musashi had once worn it in his belt that the sword was miraculously saved? Or was it saved because Sanemori had forged it with such care? It is hard to say.

The sword forged by Takada Masayuki is two feet and eight inches long and is now in the possession of Okabe Kyūsaemon [Hidetoki]. Under the hilt it has the inscription "Shinmen Musashi no Kami." During the times of [Okabe] Kadayū it was confiscated by Nagaoka Hisayuki, who passed it on to Dōke Heizō [Munenari], one of the *deshi* of Terao Motomenosuke, a direct pupil Musashi's direct pupils, and the founder of his own school of swordsmanship.

None of Musashi's swords, long or short, were finished with gold, whereas his *wakizashi* was. Swords, after all, might be put aside when visiting someone's place, and to have one's weapons inlaid with gold might give people the impressions that they were merely ornamental and their owner not prepared for the worst. His *wakizashi*, however, would never leave his belt, so it did not matter if it were ornamented with gold.

- Ōhara Sanemori was a swordsmith from Hōki and a descendant of the famous Ōhara Yasutsuna, who us believed to have been one of Japan's earliest swordsmiths.

- This is the second time Sawamura Usaemon Tomoyoshi (a senior Hosokawa retainer) makes his appearance, the first time being when Masanaga describes Musashi's life in Higo on the basis of Yamamoto Katsuyasu's *Dōsui dengen*.
- *Shimenawa* are lengths of braided rice straw used for ritual purification in Shinto religion. Thick versions of *shimenawa* can often be seen hanging from the outer beams of Shinto shrines to ward off evil spirits. They are also used to mark sacred landmarks such as trees believed to be inhabited by spirits.
- The Tsuboi district is just to the northeast of Kumamoto castle, while the Kyō district is located to the north of the castle, so that the wind must have been from the east on that fateful day.
- Toyoda Kennai is believed to be none other than Toyoda Takahisa, the grandfather of the author Toyoda Masanaga. Takahisa entered the service of Nagaoka Okinaga after his father had fallen in the suppression of the Shimabara rebellion. Takahisa, then, was already in the service of the Nagaoka by the time Musashi arrived in Higo, so that many of the anecdotes Masanaga heard about Musashi may have been passed down from his grandfather.
- Sawamura Daikurō Tomoaki (1749–1800) was the grandson of Sawamura Tomoyoshi, and the son of Sawamura Tomomasa, during whose lifetime the extraordinary incident is said to have taken place.
- Takada Masayuki was a well-known swordsmith from Bungo.
- Okabe Kyūsaemon Hidetoki entered the service of the Nagaoka when, on his deathbed in 1645, Musashi recommended Kyūsaemon to Yoriyuki. His son Okabe Kadayū Hidetake followed in his father's footsteps at the age of nine, and went on to serve three successive generations of Nagaoka chieftains: Yoriyuki, Naoyuki, and Hisayuki.

- Dōke Heizō Munenari belonged to a clan of retainers to the Hosokawa clan. His great grandfather had entered the service of Hosokawa Tadaoki in 1602, two years after the battle of Sekigahara. At that time Tadaoki was still the lord of Kokura castle, in the province of Buzen. When Tadaoki was promoted to the fiefdom of Kumamoto the Dōke followed them and were granted a fief of more than two thousand *koku*. When, in old age, Musashi settled in Kumamoto, Munenari's father, Kakusaemon, became one of his last pupils.
- Terao Motomenosuke Nobuyuki (1621–88) was a retainer of Hosokawa Tadatoshi. Along with his brother, Terao Magonojō Nobumasa (1611–72), he became one of the three men selected by Musashi to keep the Niten Ichi school of swordsmanship alive.

❧ The Mysterious Sword

Among Musashi's armor was a sword he had received from Lord Hosokawa Tadatoshi. Needless to state that the ornaments were made of solid gold. As it was an ornamental sword, Musashi attached to it a new cord to suspend it from the waist of his armor, something he did not do with any of his other swords. It always took pride of place in the alcove of his house. This was told to me by Okabe Kyūsaemon [Hidetoki].

Previously, I mentioned the sword forged by Ōhara Sanemori. Once, when a man was sentenced to death, the sword was mistakenly selected to be used in his execution. Yet when the sword was used it failed to perform as expected, even at a second and third attempt. At this the executioner said: "I know that this is such a good sword that not even a rock seems hard. Could it be that its quality is beyond my skill to handle?" Again he tried, but the result was the same as before. But when he shook off the blood and tried to sheath the sword, he could only insert it halfway into the sheath. And it was in that condition that he returned the sword to its owner.

Seeing this, Sawamura Usaemon [Tomoyoshi] said: "Why is it that this sword was selected for use? This is the very sword that has been handed down from master Musashi. It has invariably been the cause of mysteries, and the members of my household know that it is a sacred object. However, now that it has been used in a execution it has been severely tainted." Having said this, he immediately left the sword in the custody of Higo's Fujisaki Hachiman shrine, where after three weeks of diligent worship, the sword, which had hitherto resisted being either sheathed or unsheathed, could be returned to its sheath as if nothing had happened.

Aware that the sword was equal to the three foot swords of Chinese emperors, the house of Sawamura revered it all the more, and it has kept the sword stored a in a box tied down with a *shimenawa* as relic of devotion ever since. This was told to me by Toyoda Kennai [Takahisa].

According to Murakami Hachirōemon [Masayuki] one of Musashi's two *bokutō* was two feet and seven inches in length, and the other was one foot and six inches in length.

- Okabe Kyūsaemon Hidetoki entered the service of the Nagaoka on Musashi's recommendation.
- Toyoda Kennai is believed to be Toyoda Takahisa, the grandfather of the author Toyoda Masanaga. Takahisa entered the service of Nagaoka Okinaga after his father had fallen in the suppression of the Shimabara rebellion.

- Masanaga specifies the length of the two *bokutō* in *shaku*, the traditional Japanese standard of measurement. The long *bokutō* is two *shaku* and seven *sun* in length, and the short *bokutō* is one *shaku*, six *sun*, and two *bu* in length. Over the centuries the size of the *shaku* has differed, even from region to region, giving rise to different names, such as the *kanejaku*, the *kujirajaku*, and the *gofukujaku*. During the Meiji period (1868–1912), however, the *shaku* was standardized, in that the *kanejaku* was adopted as the national unit of measurement at 33.303 cm, or just under one foot. Unlike the foot, the *shaku* is divided into ten units instead of twelve to arrive at the Japanese equivalent of the inch, which is called a *sun*. The *sun*, in turn, is divided into ten *bu*.

- Murakami Hachirōemon Masayuki seems to have been a swordsman in the service of the Toyoda clan and a practitioner of Musashi's Niten Ichi-ryū. Following the author's death, he became the personal fencing instructor to Masanaga's son, Toyoda Kagehide, the author of the *Nitenki*.

❷ Aoki Jōemon

Aoki Jōemon, who was later called Tetsujin, was a *deshi* of Musashi and an accomplished practitioner of the art of fencing with two swords. He is mentioned in the *Honchō bugei shoden.*

It also speaks of the Miyamoto Musashi Seimei-ryū, and says that Musashi's father was called Munisai, that he was an adept with the *jitte,* and that his school of Swordsmanship was called the Nihon Kaizan Enmei Miyamoto Musashi Seimei-ryū. Yet though I have recorded the Kokura monument epitaph, there is no mention of this name in the text. Surely it is an error in the *Honchō bugei shoden.*

- According to the *Bushū denraiki* Aoki had formerly been a *deshi* of Musashi's father, from whom he had received teaching in the Tōri school of swordsmanship.

🌀 Togō Tabei

According to Musashi's direct *deshi* Dōke Kakusaemon, once, in one of his their conversations, Musashi mentioned that he knew many people but that he had never met a man with such courage as Togō Tabei and that he was the kind of man who faced things without changing his heart.

In June of the fourth year of Shōho [July, 1647] a Portuguese galleon arrived in the port of Nagasaki. Our lord sent troops by ship and Togō was among the men who had embarked. Among them, too, was Nagaoka Kenmotsu [Koretaka] and his son Samanojō (who later took the Buddhist name of Jūan), while the latter was attended on by Sakamoto Iemon. They sought to bar the ship from reaching open sea by constructing a bridge across the entrance of the narrow bay where it was moored. According to master Jūan it was hard to tell whether any of the men from Kumamoto wanted to return home, or whether they were prepared to offer their lives wholeheartedly. All of them, whether they were of firm character or cowards, seemed to have lost their usual fighting spirit, being merely carried along in the excitement. The only one among them who had not changed from his usual self was Togō Tabei.

Such, too, was the purport of Musashi's teachings: to face things without changing one's heart. Truly, Togō Tabei was a stout man of such a disposition.

- Togō Tabei was a warrior who had entered the service of the Hosokawa in the 1620s, prior to the clan's move to Kumamoto. He had become the page of Hosokawa Tadatoshi, at that time still the master of Moji castle in Buzen. In the siege of Hara castle during the suppression of the Shimabara Rebellion, he had been one of the first men to reach the castle's inner ring, a feat that earned him a stipend of 300 *koku*. Toward the end of his military career he was in charge of a regiment of musketeers. He retired from military life in 1674.
- Nagaoka Kenmotsu Korekata (1586–1658) was an elder of the Hosokawa in Kumamoto. In his youth he had served Tadaoki, but in 1614 he joined Toyotomi Hideyori at Osaka castle. Hideyori's defeat forced him to lie low for a while, but in 1622 he was accepted back into the service of the Hosokawa at the age of thirty-seven. He soon climbed in rank, increasing his fief from two thousand to more than six thousand *koku* within three years until, by 1634 he had reached the position of senior retainer with a fief of ten thousand *koku*.

❧ Terao Motomenosuke

Terao Motomenosuke Nobuyuki (who was later called Shichirōemon) had five sons: Sakai (who succeeded his father as commander of a regiment of musketeers and inherited the family fief of three hundred *koku*); Yoshinosuke (who became a middle-rank page); Kaganosuke (who was dispatched to Shingumi; but later deserted); Benkai Nobuaki (who was later called Shinmen Nobumori); and Wanuinosuke (who also became a middle-rank page and was later renamed Gōemon). All this I have learned from master Murakami Hachirōemon Masayuki.

- Murakami Hachirōemon Masayuki seems to have been a swordsman in the service of the Toyoda clan and a practitioner of Musashi's Niten Ichi-ryū. Following the author's death, he became the personal fencing instructor to Masanaga's son, Toyoda Kagehide, the author of the *Nitenki.*

❷ The *Deshi* of the Terao Brothers

Among Terao Motomenosuke [Nobuyuki's] *deshi* was Koshino Jirōemon, Dōke Heizō [Munenari], and Murakami Hirauchi [Masahide]. All three of them were Motomenosuke's immediate successors, initiated into the inner secrets of the Niten Ichi school of swordsmanship. Beside them were Matoba Jinemon, Watanabe Shinnojō, Oku Kyūemon, and Naoshita Gentabei, all of them men who belonged to the group who inherited [part of] Musashi's teachings.

Among the *deshi* of Terao Magonojō [Nobumasa] were Yamamoto Gennosuke [Katsuhide] (Dosui's son, who was later called Gensaemon); Inoue Kakubei Masatsugu (whose Buddhist name was Soken, and who inherited the *Book of Five Rings* in August of the seventh year of Kanbun [September 1667] after he had become Magonojō's chosen successor); Nakayama Heemon Masakatsu (whose Buddhist name was Miken), Tsutsumi Tsugubei Nagamichi (whose later name was Matasaemon and whose Buddhist name was Issui); as well as a host of other men who were generally initiated into the secrets of Musashi's Niten Ichi-ryū and who had practiced the art of fencing with two swords from the very start. (It was from Tsutsumi Tsugubei Nagamichi that I inherited the introduction to the five laws [*Book of Five Rings*]).

Terao Magonojō did not teach only one generation in the art of swordsmanship. Lord Chikugo, Yamana Jūsaemon, Uragami Jūbei, and Shibatō Sanzaemon all were among his *deshi*. Terao Motomenosuke's descendants, too, continue to practice Musashi's art of swordsmanship unbroken. Among his five sons Benkai [Nobuaki] exceeded his brother Kaganosuke in skill.

Copied by Tamura Hideyuki on an auspicious day of June of the second year of Bunsei [July 1819].

- Koshino Jirōemon's ancestors had entered the service of Hosokawa Tadaoki at the turn of the sixteenth century in return for a fief of three hundred *koku*. That fief was inherited by Jirōemon in 1686, when his father took the tonsure and retired from active service. It seems that Jirōemon did well, for when, in 1713, Jirōemon passed away himself, the family fief had been increased threefold to nine hundred *koku*.

- Dōke Heizō Munenari's grandfather had entered the service of Hosokawa Tadaoki in 1602 in return for a fief of one thousand *koku*. At that time Tadaoki was still the lord of Kokura castle, in the province of Buzen. When Tadaoki was promoted to the fiefdom of Kumamoto the Dōke followed them and their fief was doubled to two thousand *koku*. Being a second son, Munenari's father, Kakusaemon, did not inherit the family fief, but was hired in return for a fief with a yield of only two hundred *koku*. As Masanaga describes, Kakusaemon was to become one of Musashi's direct *deshi*, following the latter's move to Kumamoto. When Kakusaemon retired in 1691, his fief went to Munenari, who served the Hosokawa until his death following a short illness in 1712.

- Murakami Hirauchi Masahide's grandfather, Masashige, also entered the service of the Hosokawa clan at the turn of the sixteenth century, when he became the page of Hosokawa Tadatoshi on a stipend of two hundred *koku*. During the suppression of the Shimabara Rebellion, Masashige was hit by a bullet and died soon afterward at the age of thirty-three. Consequently, Masashige's son (and Masahide's father), Masayuki, was only six when he inherited his family's fief of two hundred *koku* in 1637.

  Ten years later, at the age of only sixteen, Masayuku was one of the many men to participate in the attempt to capture the Portuguese galleon. It did not serve to increase his position, for when he retired and passed on his possessions to Masahide, the yield of the family fief was still two hundred *koku*. It might have been out of dissatisfaction that, in 1694, at the age of twenty-nine.

  Masahide sought to leave the service of the Hosokawa to pursue a life of *musha shugyō*. His request, however, was turned down and it was probably out of punishment that three years later his properties were confiscated and that he was forced to take up life as a subsistence farmer in the vicinity of Sakuchi, some ten miles north of Kumamoto.

- Matoba Jinemon's great grandfather had entered the service of the Hosokawa clan in return for a fief of three hundred *koku*. Both his eldest son and his grandson passed away at a young age, so that the family fief was passed on to an adopted son, Jinemon's father, Kinemon. Like many of his peers, Jinemon came into his family possessions toward the end of the seventeenth century when, in 1693, his older brother passed away only four years after his father had taken the tonsure and gone into retirement.

- Watanabe Shinnojō's ancestors hailed from Harima, where they had been in the service of the Akamatsu clan. Shinjirō's father had been the first to enter the service of the

Hosokawa, under whom he served in the suppression of the Shimabara rebellion. Shinjirō followed in his father's footsteps when, in 1679, he became the page of Tadatoshi's grandson, Hosokawa Tsunatoshi. He died in 1691, having occupied a number of different posts and leaving behind a fief of three hundred *koku*.

- Oku Kyūemon's grandfather, Jirōsaemon, entered the service of Hosokawa Tadatoshi in the 1630s on a fief of two hundred *koku*. It seems that Jirōsaemon's offspring was not endowed with a firm constitution, for both he and his son passed away at a young age, leaving the family fief of two hundred *koku* to Kyūemon who was then (1687) still only fifteen years old. Kyūemon served Hosokawa Tsunatoshi in a number of capacities, including that of caretaker of the clan's Edo premises, before he took the tonsure in 1740.

- Naoshita Gentabei's grandfather, Shichinosuke, entered the service of Hosokawa Tadaoki on a fief of three hundred *koku*. His oldest daughter became one of Tadaoki's concubines and gave birth to a son who would be adopted by Nagaoka Okinaga and given the name Yoriyuki. Shichinosuke was to serve three generations of Hosokawa chieftains until he passed away in 1655. His second son (and Gentabei's father), Shichibei, was only fourteen at that time. By the time Shichibei went into retirement and passed on the family fief to Gentabei in 1698, he had served the Hosokawa for almost half a century. Gentabei served the Hosokawa in a number of posts until, in 1734, he, too, took the tonsure and went into retirement.

- Yamamoto Gennosuke Katsuhide was the son of Yamamoto Gengosaemon Katsuyasu (Dosui) a retainer of the Nagaoka and one of Musashi's *deshi*. His father, who was the keeper of Yatsushiro castle, held a fief of seven hundred *koku*. When Katsuyasu fell ill and died, the fief did not go to his son, but to his brother, Kaneshige.

- Inoue Kakubei Masatsugu's father had entered the service of the Nagaoka clan in return for a fief of seven hundred *koku*. Masatsugu followed in his father's footsteps when, in 1665, he became the page of Nagaoka Naoyuki. Later in life, Masatsugu became the private fencing instructor to Naoyuki's son, Tameyuki.

- Nakayama Heemon Masakatsu, too, entered the service of Nagaoka Naoyuki early in the 1660s as a page. At that stage his stipend was only forty *koku*, but he quickly climbed in rank, gaining his own fief of two hundred *koku* in 1679. He went on to occupy a string of different posts, including that of head of archers and head of musketeers until, in 1713, he took the tonsure and went into retirement.

- Tsutsumi Tsugubei Nagamichi's father, Nagamasa, had entered the service of Hosokawa Tadatoshi's brother, Tatsutaka in 1632, but was forced to take up subsistence farming when his master died. Things improved for the Tsutsumi when, in 1655, at the age of fifteen, Nagamichi entered the service of the Nagaoka as a page to the young Naoyuki. Nagamichi was to serve the Nagaoka for close to half a century. By the time he took the tonsure in 1701 at the age of sixty-one, he had become one of their most trusted retainers.

- Lord Chikugo is the honorary name of Nagaoka Naoyuki.

- Yamana Jūsaemon was the grandson of Nagaoka Umanusuke Shigemasa, one of the men who attended the renga meetings with Musashi.

- Uragami Jūbei was a retainer of the Hosokawa clan.

- Shibatō Sanzaemon Yoshinori (1629–1710), too, was a Hosokawa retainer at the time he studied under Musashi. Following Musashi's death he moved to Chikuzen, where he entered the service of Kuroda Mitsuyuki (1628–1707) as head of pages and fencing instructor, thus founding the Fukuoka strand of the Niten Ichi school of swordsmanship. Later in life he moved to Akashi, in Harima, where he was to impart his knowledge of Musashi's school of swordsmanship to Tanji Hōkin, the author of the *Bushū denraiki.*

Old Provinces

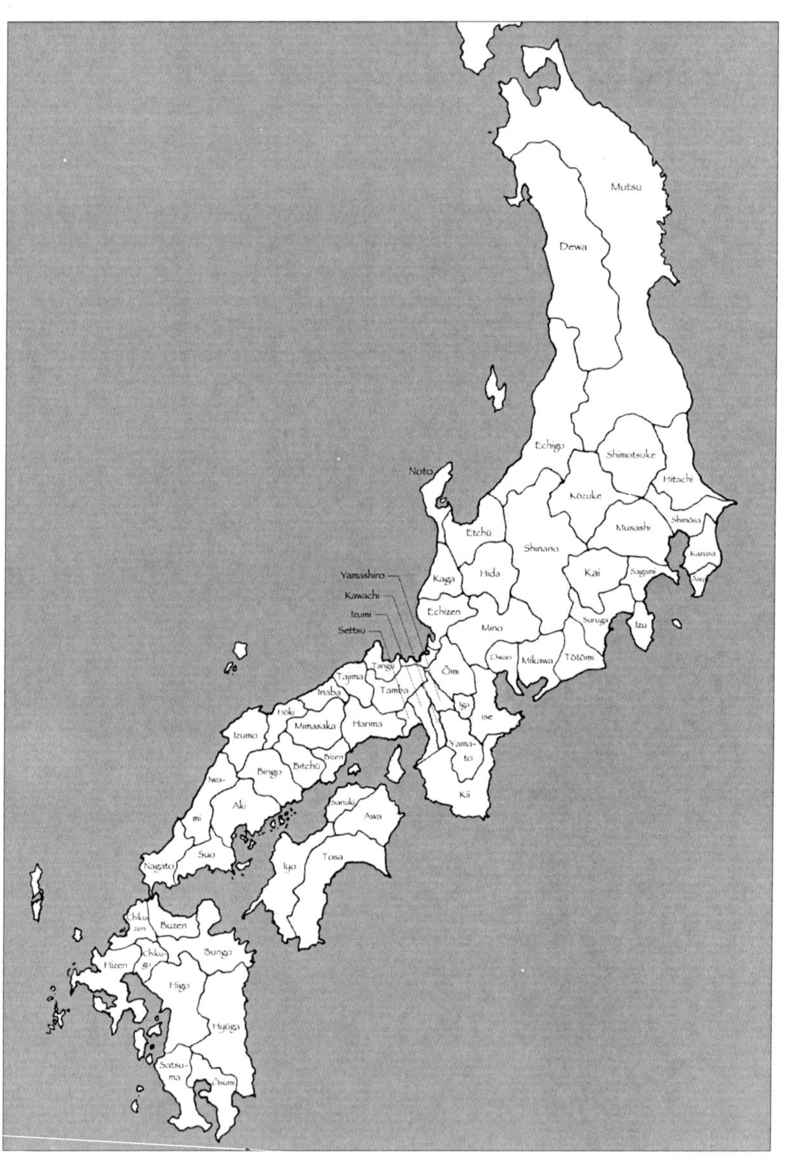

❀ Old Provinces and Their Modern Equivalents

Aki:	Hiroshima		Kazusa:	Chiba
Awa:	Tokushima		Kii:	Wakayama
Bingo:	Hiroshima		Kōzuke:	Gunma
Bitchū:	Okayama		Mikawa:	Aichi
Bizen:	Okayama		Mimasaka:	Okayama
Bungo:	Ōita		Mino:	Gifu
Buzen:	Fukuoka		Musashi:	Saitama and Tokyo
Chikugo:	Fukuoka		Mutsu:	Aomori
Chikuzen:	Fukuoka		Nagato:	Yamaguchi
Dewa:	Yamagata, Akita		Noto:	Ishikawa
Echigo:	Niigata		Ōmi:	Shiga
Echizen:	Fukui		Ōsumi:	Kagoshima
Etchū:	Fukuyama		Owari:	Aichi
Harima:	Hyōgo		Sagami:	Kanagawa
Hida:	Gifu		Sanuki:	Kagawa
Higo:	Kumamoto		Satsuma:	Kagoshima
Hitachi:	Ibaraki		Settsu:	Osaka
Hizen:	Nagasaki		Shimōsa:	Chiba
Hōki:	Tottori		Shinano:	Nagano
Hyūga:	Miyazaki		Suō:	Yamaguchi
Iga:	Mie		Suruga:	Shizuoka
Inaba:	Tottori		Tajima:	Hyōgo
Ise:	Mie		Tamba:	Kyoto
Iwami:	Shimane		Tango:	Kyoto
Iyo:	Ehime		Tosa:	Kōchi
Izu:	Shizuoka		Tōtōmi:	Shizuoka
Izumi:	Osaka		Wakasa:	Fukui
Izumo:	Shimane		Yamashiro:	Kyoto
Kaga:	Ishikawa		Yamato:	Nara
Kai:	Yamanashi			
Kawachi:	Osaka			

Castles, Temples, and Shrines

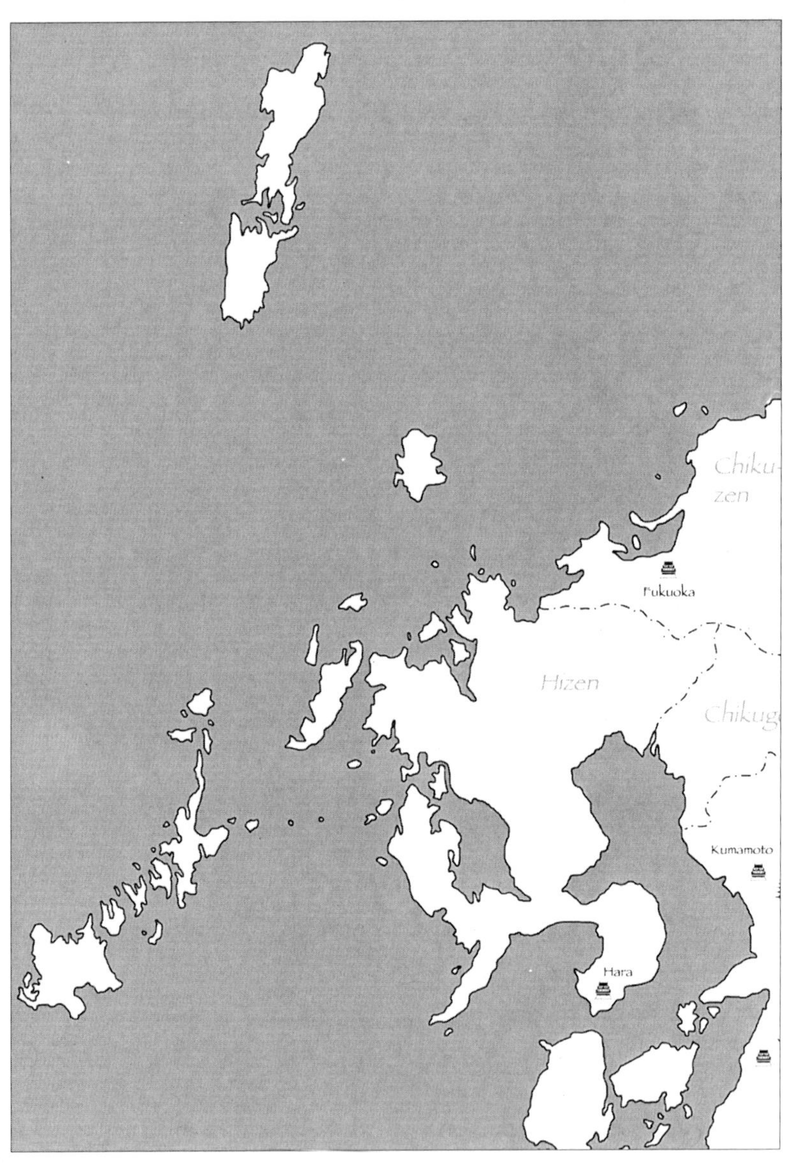

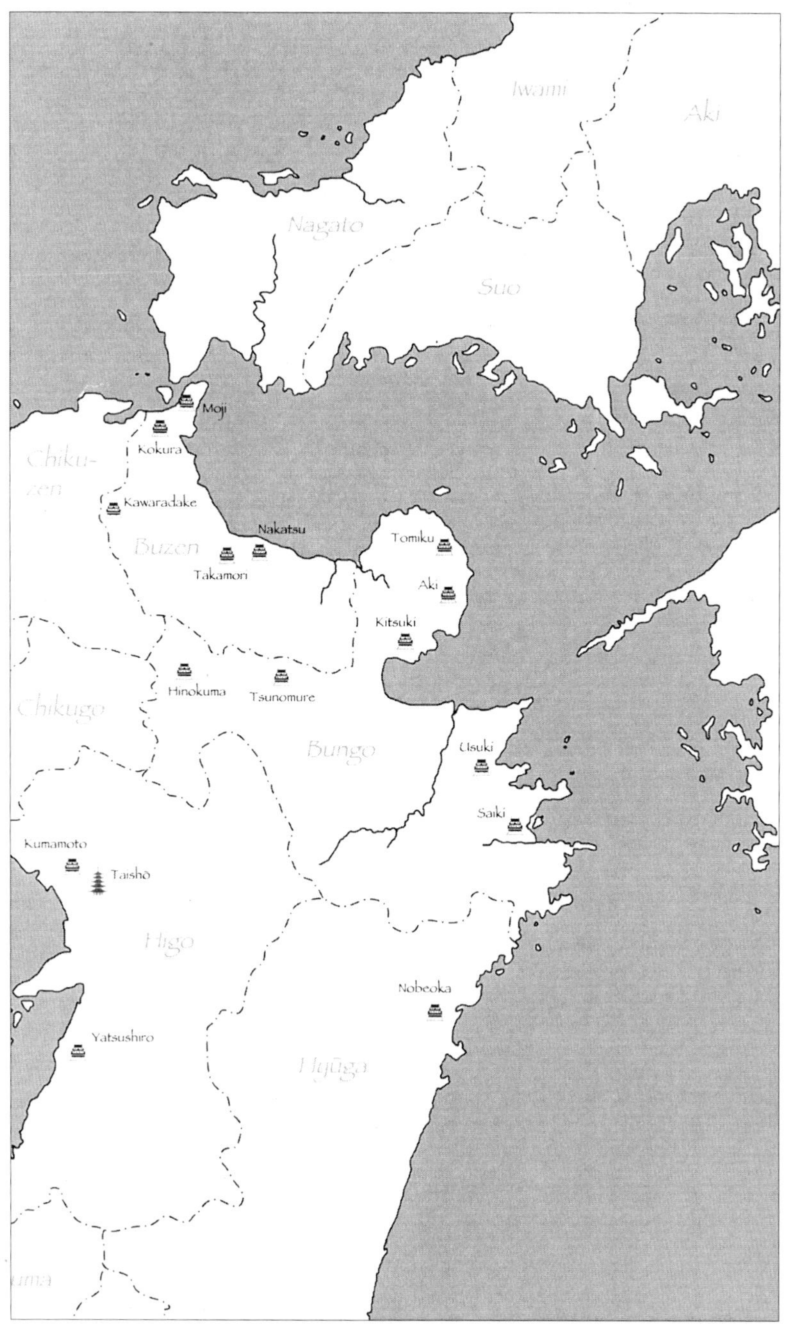

Iwami
Aki
Nagato
Suo
Moji
Kokura
Chiku-
zen
Kawaradake
Buzen
Nakatsu
Tomiku
Takamori
Aki
Kitsuki
Hinokuma
Tsunomure
Chikugo
Bungo
Usuki
Saiki
Kumamoto
Taishō
Higo
Yatsushiro
Nobeoka
Hyūga
uma

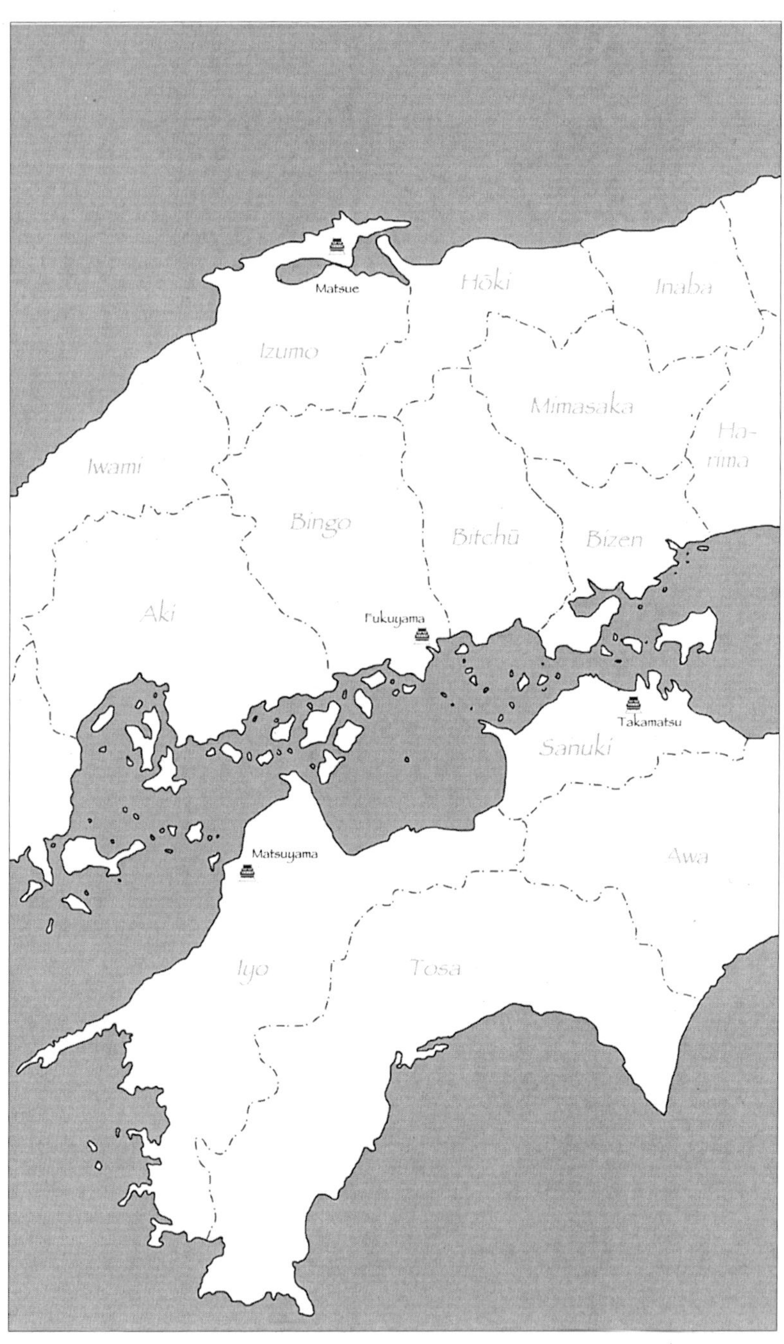

Matsue
Izumo
Hōki
Inaba
Iwami
Mimasaka
Ha-
rima
Bingo
Bitchū
Bizen
Aki
Fukuyama
Takamatsu
Sanuki
Matsuyama
Awa
Iyo
Tosa

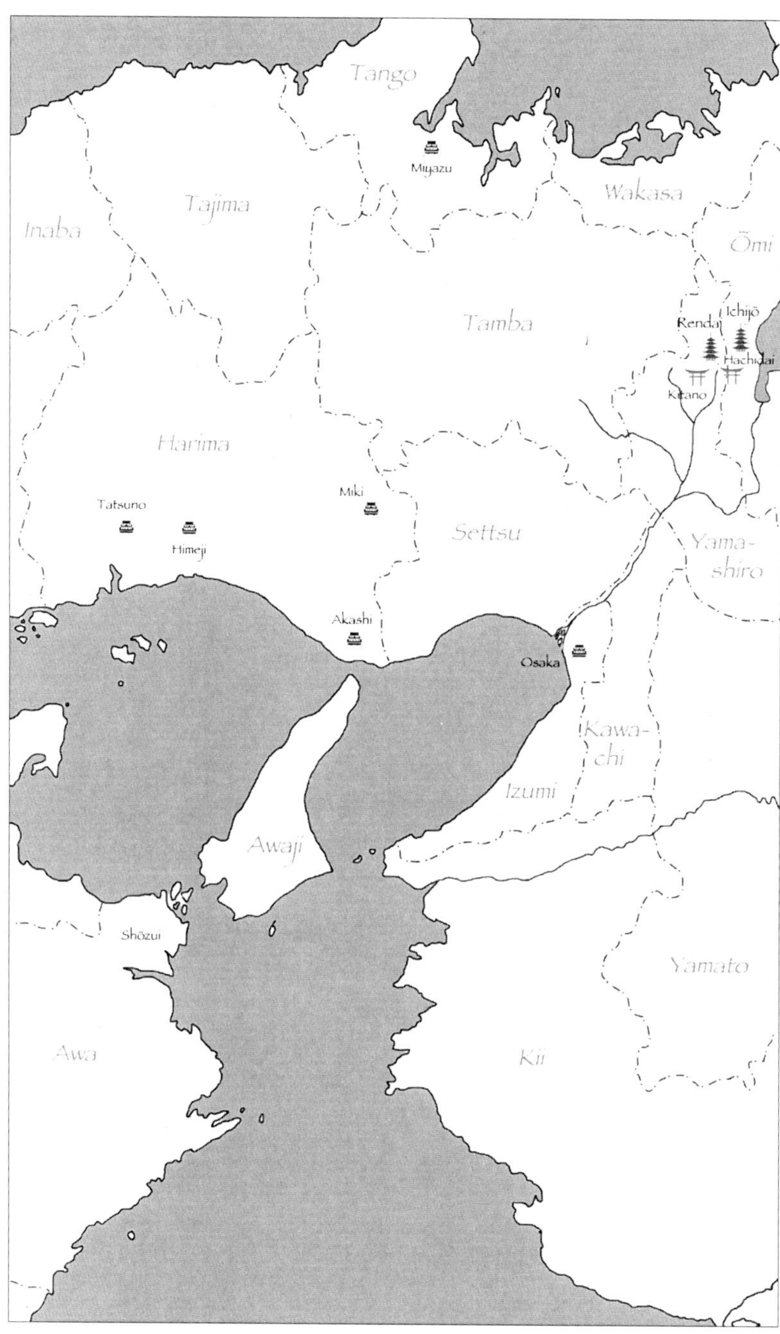

Tango
Miyazu
Wakasa
Tajima
Inaba
Ōmi
Tamba
Ichijō
Renda
Hachidai
Kitano
Harima
Miki
Tatsuno
Settsu
Himeji
Yama-
shiro
Akashi
Osaka
Kawa-
chi
Izumi
Awaji
Yamato
Shōzui
Awa
Kii

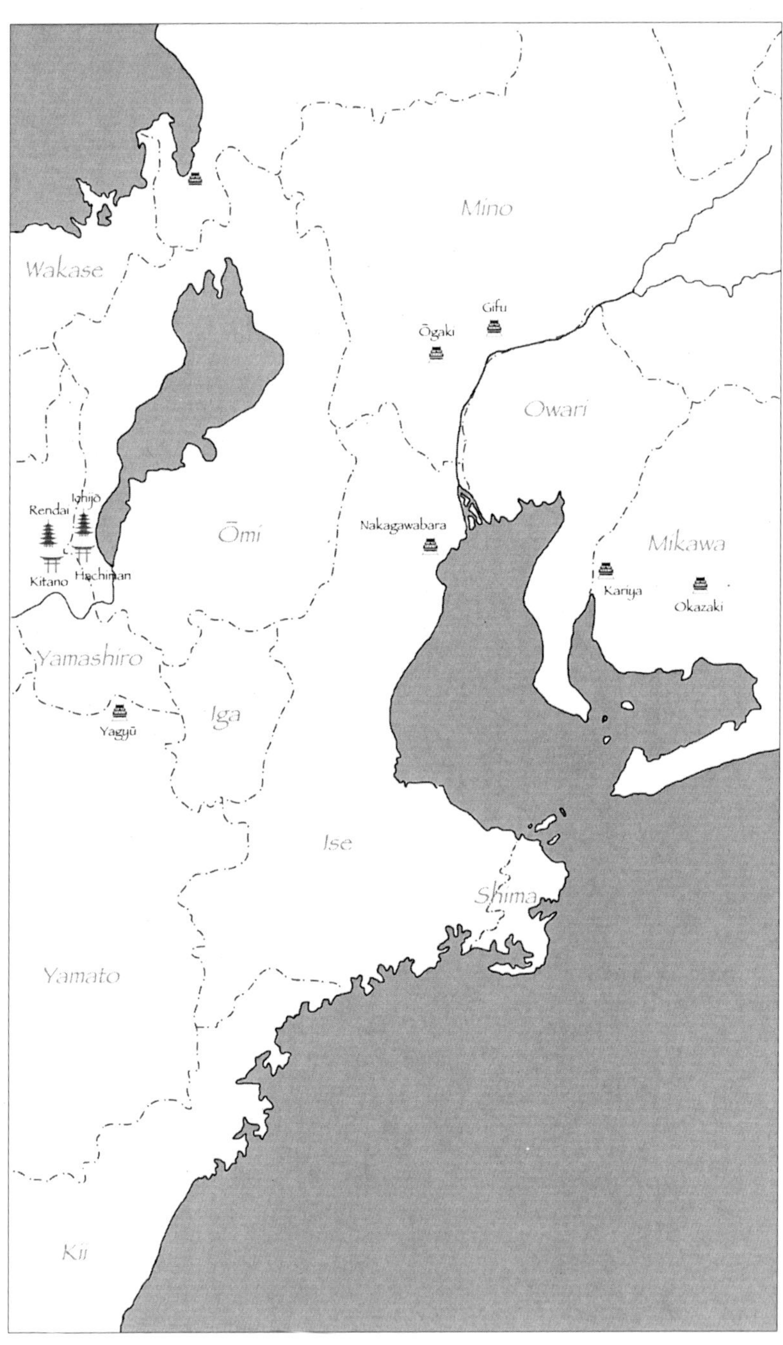
Wakase
Mino
Gifu
Ōgaki
Owari
Rendai
Ichijō
Ōmi
Nakagawabara
Mikawa
Kitano
Hachiman
Kariya
Okazaki
Yamashiro
Iga
Yagyū
Ise
Shima
Yamato
Kii

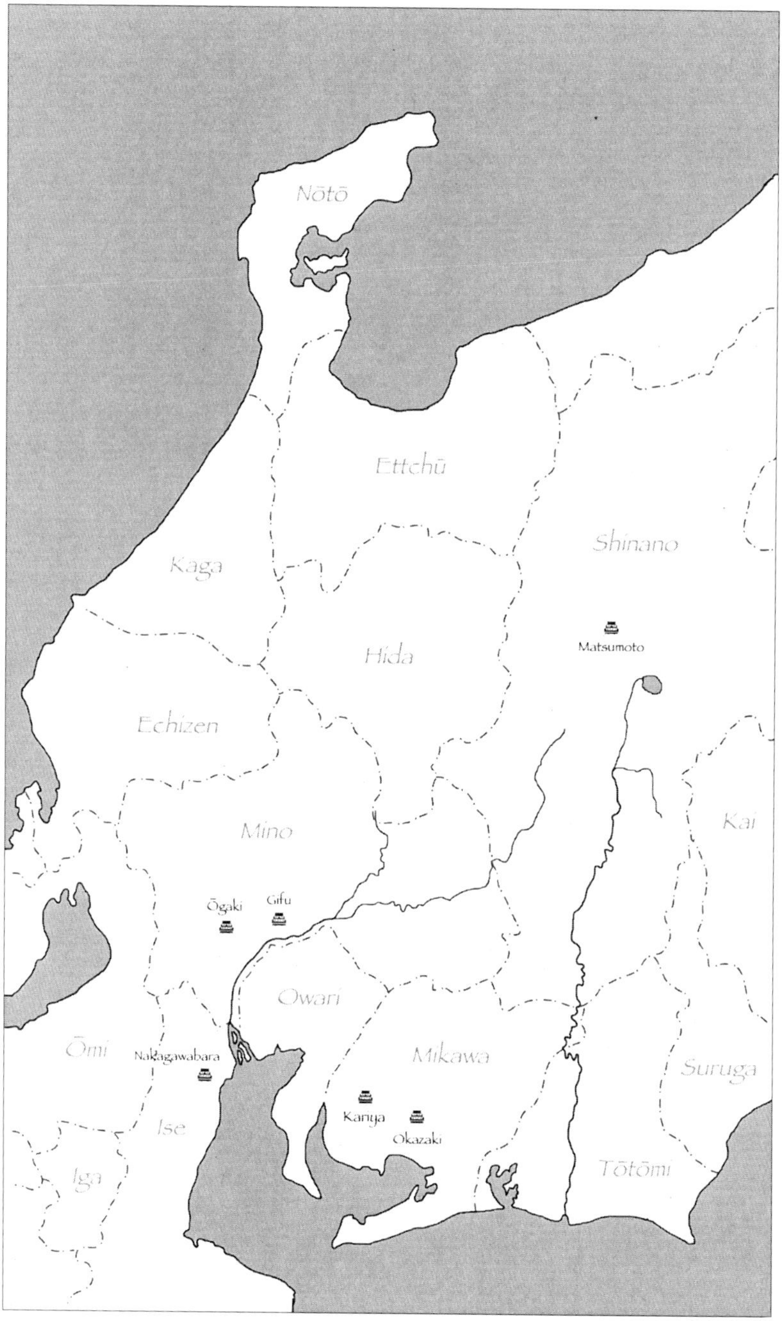

Notō
Ettchū
Shinano
Kaga
Hida
Matsumoto
Echizen
Kai
Mino
Ōgaki
Gifu
Owari
Ōmi
Nakagawabara
Mikawa
Suruga
Ise
Kariya
Okazaki
Iga
Tōtōmi

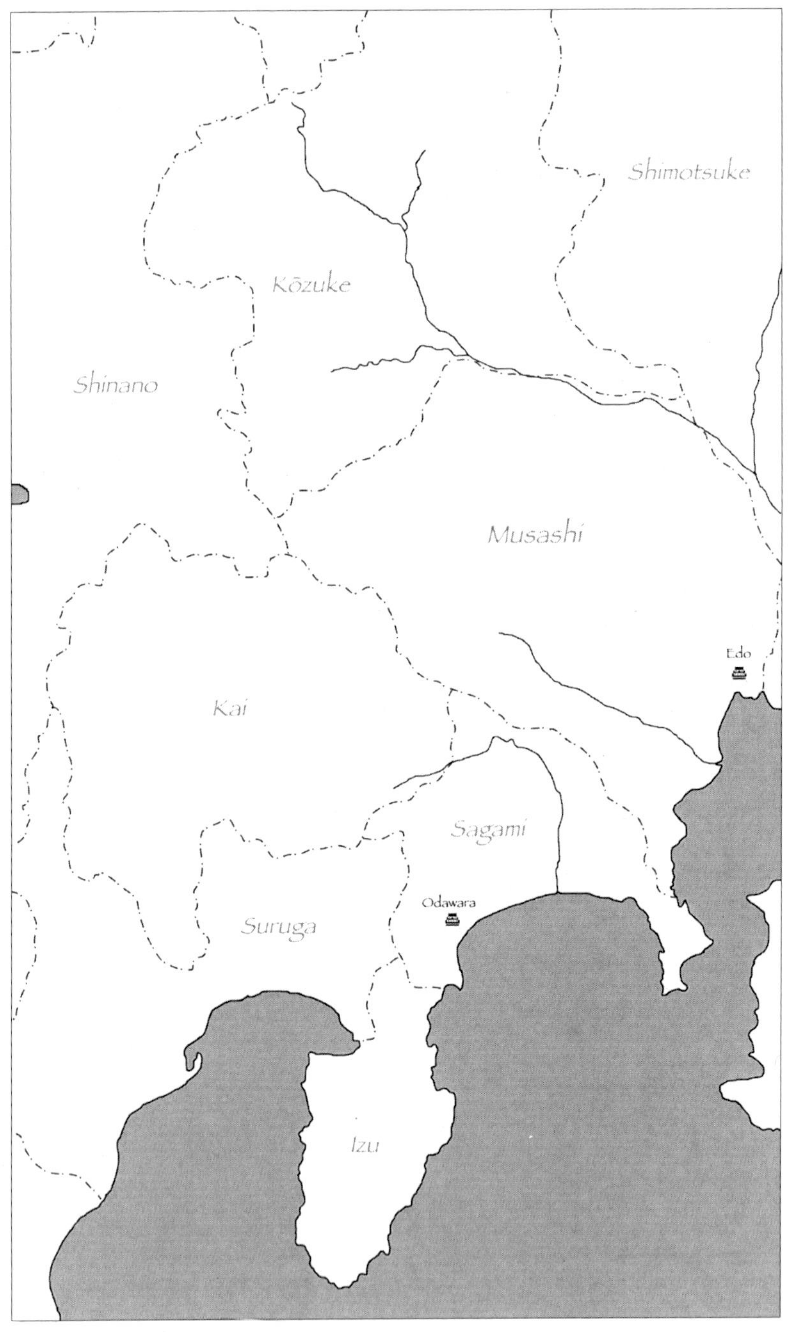
Shimotsuke
Kōzuke
Shinano
Musashi
Edo
Kai
Sagami
Odawara
Suruga
Izu

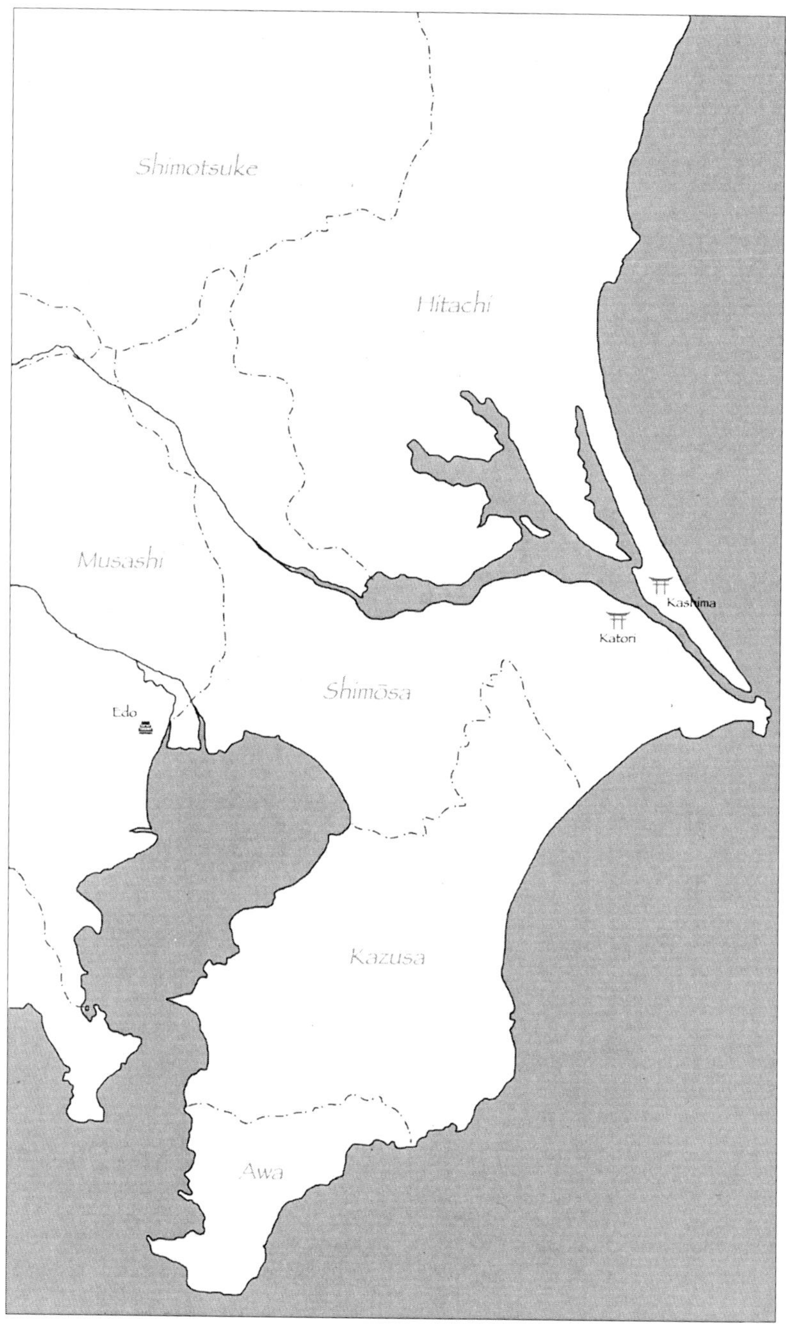

Shimotsuke
Hitachi
Musashi
Kashima
Katori
Edo
Shimōsa
Kazusa
Awa

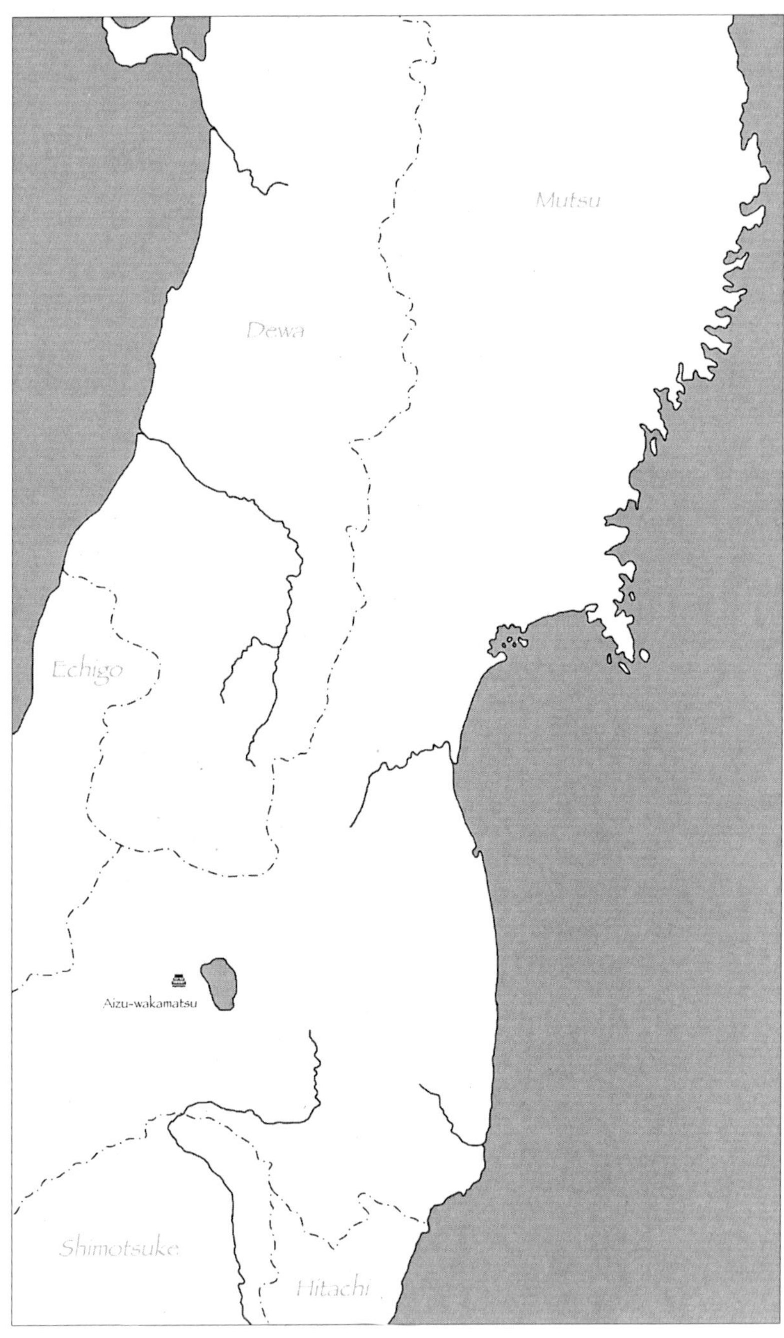

Mutsu
Dewa
Echigo
Aizu-wakamatsu
Shimotsuke
Hitachi

Important Castles

Akashi castle:	Headquarters of Ogasawara Tadazane, who hired Musashi as an adviser during the construction of Akashi castle.
Aki castle:	One of the many castles subdued by Kuroda Yoshitaka during his campaign against the forces of Ōtomo Yoshimune.
Fukuoka castle:	Headquarters of the Kuroda clan during the second half of Musashi's life. It was under the control of Kuroda Tadayuki by the time Musashi went into retirement.
Hara castle:	Center of the Shimabara Rebellion in which Musashi saw action as the guardian of Ogasawara Nagatsugu.
Himeji castle:	Headquarters of Honda Tadatoki, the lord of Musashi's first adoptive son, Mikinosuke.
Kitsuki castle:	First castle to come under the attack of Ōtomo Yoshimune, before he was ousted by Musashi's lord, Kuroda Yoshitaka.
Kokura castle:	Initially the headquarters of Hosokawa Tadatoki, but following his promotion to Kumamoto castle, the seat of the Ogasawara clan, during whose reign Musashi often visited the castle.
Kumamoto castle:	Headquarters of the Hosokawa Tadatoshi, the man who allowed Musashi to retire to what had once been the residential quarters of the local Ideta clan.
Matsuyama castle:	Location of the residence of Matsudaira Katsutaka, the Bakufu official who challenged Musashi to a duel in the garden of his library.
Moji castle:	Headquarters of Hosokawa Tadatoshi dur-

ing Musashi's legendary duel with Sasaki Kojirō on Ganryū island.

Nakatsu castle: Headquarters of Kuroda Yoshitaka when Musashi joined his father in Takamori.

Takamori castle: Headquarters of the Kuroda clan during the first half of Musashi's life.

Yatsushiro castle: Headquarters of Nagaoka Okinaga, who prevailed on Musashi to leave the Reigan cave and spend his last days at what had once been the quarters of the local Ideta clan.

Important Temples

Hōkō temple:	Situated in Kyoto and the place where Yoshioka Kenpō got embroiled in a fight and was killed by the assembled guards.
Ichijō temple:	Situated east of Kyoto and the place where Musashi is believed to have duelled with members of the Yoshioka clan.
Rendai tempel:	Situated in Kyoto and according to Hōkin the place where Musashi duelled with Yoshioka Seijūrō.
Taishō temple:	The Hosokawa family temple in Kumamoto, led by Akiyama Wanao, one of Musashi close friends in old age.
Yōjū temple:	Situated just south of Kumamoto castle, on the northern bank of the Shira river and once the location of Musashi's mortuary tablet (wich was later moved to the grounds of the Taigan temple, where it was destroyed by fire as a result of Allied bombings).

Important Shrines

Hachidai shrine:	One of the possible shrines Musashi passed on his way to his duel with Yoshioka Matashichirō, it is situated only a few hundred meters away from the Ichijō temple.
Kitano Hachiman:	One of the possible shrines Musashi passed on his way to his duel with Yoshioka Mataschichirō, it is situated west of Kyoto, and equally near an area of the city that is still called Kudarimatsu

Historical Periods

Japan

Nara	710–94
Heian	794–1185
Kamakura	1185–1333
Muromachi	1333–1568
Momoyama	1568–1600
Tokugawa	1600–1868

China

Han	202 bc–ad 220
Three Kingdoms	221–65
Six Dynasties	265–581
Sui	581–618
Tang	618–906
Five Dynasties	907–60
Northern Song	960–1127
Southern Song	1127–1279
Yuan	1271–1368
Ming	1368–1644
Qing	1644–1911

Periods of Military Rule

Kamakura Bakufu	1185–1333
Muromachi Bakufu (Ashikaga Bakufu)	1333–1568
Edo Bakufu (Tokugawa Bakufu)	1603–1867

Battles and Rebellions

Battles

Rebellions

 Glossary

ashigaru:	Foot soldier.
bokutō:	Wooden sword used for practice.
bun-bu:	Used to refer to a warrior's civil and martial accomplishments.
daimyō:	Feudal lord.
denki:	Biography.
deshi:	Pupil or desciple of a master of an art or craft who has comitted him- or herself to study the art or craft in question for a number of years.
go-tairō:	Council of Five Regents.
hakama:	Trousered skirt, worn by the samurai.
haori:	Lightweight silk jacket originally meant to be worn by men as a component of the *hakama*
hatamoto:	Direct retainer or "bannerman" of the shōgun.
hatasashi:	Medieval heraldic banner.
heihō:	Art or method of warfare, here generally employed to mean the martial arts.
heihōsha:	Practitioner of the art of *heihō*.
hoshu jutsu:	Compendium of siezing, holding, and binding techniques that were employed to arrest culprits or deal with those who had been captured alive during siege warfare.
jitte:	A traditional weapon consisting of an iron rod that may vary in length between thirty centimeters to a meter with a fork-like extension situated just above the hilt.
jūjutsu:	Bare-handed form of combat art based on a variety of grapling techniques.
karusan hakama:	*Hakama* with trouser legs that tapered toward the lower end so that they sat tight round the lower shins.

koku:	Medieval unit of measurement, approximately 180 liters. Here it is used to express the anual rice yield of a plot of land, one *koku* being sufficient to keep a man alive for a year.
kosode:	Generic name for either a lower-class outer garment or an upper-class undergarment.
musha bugyō:	Magistrate of Warriors.
musha shugyō:	Literarlly, "warrior training" but in the context of *budō*, the old practice of ascetic self-discipline that goes back to the ancient traditions of the so-called *yamabushi*, or enigmatic mountian monks.
naginata:	Pole sword.
rōnin:	Masterless samurai.
renga:	Series of short verses that are linked into one single poem through a collaborative effort.
sakuji bugyō:	Administrator responsible for building and repairs.
sashimono:	Medieval heraldic banner.
shaku:	Japanese foot.
shiai:	Contest between two martial artists.
shimenawa:	Lengths of braided rice straw used for ritual purification in Shinto religion.
shinken:	Real sword.
shoshidai:	Deputy governor of the Samurai Dokoro.
tachi:	Longest of the pair of swords traditionally worn by samurai.
tantō:	Short dagger.
uchidachi:	The senior sparring partner when practicing *kata*. The junior sparring partner is called *shidachi*.
wakizashi:	Shortest of the pair of swords traditionally worn by samurai.
yari:	Spear or lance.
yashiki:	Medieval nobleman's mansion.
zōei bugyō:	Construction Magistrate.

 Bibliography

🌀 Works in English

Adolphson, Mikael S. *The Gates of Power*. Honolulu, 2000.

—. *The Teeth and Claws of the Buddha*. Honolulu, 2007.

Carroll, John. *Lightning in the Void*. New York, 2006.

Cleary, Thomas. *Code of the Samurai*. Tokyo, 1999.

De Lange, William. *Famous Japanese Swordsmen*, Vols. 1–3. Warren, 2008.

—. *Iaidō*, Boston, 2002.

Dening, Walter. *Japan in Days of Yore*. London, 1976.

Friday, Karl F. *Hired Swords*. 1992.

—. *Legacies of the Sword*. 1997.

Hiroaki Satō. *Legends of the Samurai*. New York, 1995.

Jansen, Marius. *Warrior Rule in Japan*. Cambridge, 2008.

Kaufman, Stephen F. *Musashi's Book of Five Rings*. New York, 2004.

Miyamoto Musashi. *The Book of Five Rings*. Translated by Bradford J. Brown. Toronto, 1982.

Miyamoto Musashi. *The Book of Five Rings*. Translated by William Scott Wilson. Tokyo. 2002.

Miyamoto Musashi. *The Book of Five Rings*. Translated by D.E. Tarver. Lincoln, 2002.

Miyamoto Musashi. *The Book of Five Rings*. Translated by Thomas Cleary. Boston, 2000.

Turnbull, S.R. *The Samurai*. New York, 1977.

Sansom, George. *A History of Japan*. Vols 1–3. Tokyo, 1963.

Sato Hiroaki. *Legends of the Samurai*. New York, 1995.

—. *The Sword and the Mind*. New York, 1985.

Sōhō Takuan, *The Unfettered Mind*. Translated by William Scott Wilson. Tokyo, 1986.

Stone, Justin F. *Bushido*. New York, 2001.

Sugawara Makoto. *Lives of Master Swordsmen*. Tokyo, 1982.

Tokitsu Kenji. *Miyamoto Musashi.* Boston, 2005.

Turnbull. S.R. *The Samurai.* New York, 1977.

—. Warriors of Medieval Japan. New York, 2005.

—. *Warriors of Japan.* Honolulu, 1994.

Varley, Paul. *Warriors of Japan.* Honolulu, 1994.

Wilson, William Scott. *Ideals of the Samurai.* Burbank, 1982.

—. *The Lone Samurai.* Tokyo, 2004.

Yamamoto Tsunetomo. *Hagakure.* Translated by William Scott Wilson. Tokyo. 1979.

Yoshikawa Eiji. *Musashi.* Tokyo, 1995.

☷ Works in Japanese

Abe Takeshi. *Sengoku jinmei jiten.* Tokyo, 1990.

Dōmon Fuyuji. *Miyamoto Musashi no jinseikun.* Tokyo, 2000.

Domoto Akihiko. *Kendō kojutsu-shi.* Tokyo, 1988.

Ezaki Junpei. *Nihon kengō retsuden.* Tokyo, 1970.

—. *Yagyū Munenori.* Tokyo, 1971.

Fukuda Akira. *Chūsei katarimono bungei.* Tokyo, 1981.

Fukuda Masahide. *Bushū denraiki.* Tokyo, 2005.

Fukuhara Josen. *Miyamoto Iori no gisho.* Okayama, 1984.

—. *Miyamoto Musashi no tankyū.* Okayama, 1978.

Futaki Kenichi. *Gassen no butaiura.* Tokyo, 1976.

Harada Mukashi. *Shinsetsu Miyamoto Musashi.* Tokyo, 1984.

Hasegawa Shin. *Nihon adauchi isō.* Tokyo, 1974.

Hayashiya Tatsusaburō. *Chūsei geinoshi no kenkyū.* Tokyo, 1960.

Hinatsu Shigetaka. *Honchō bugei shoden.* Tokyo, 2001.

Hioki Shōichi. *Nihon sōhei kenkyū.* Tokyo, 1972.

Hirotani Yūtarō. *Nihon kendō shiryō.* Tokyo, 1943.

Ichikawa Kakuji. *Miyamoto Musashi.* Tokyo, 1985.

Imai Masayuki. *Niten Ichi-ryū seihō.* Tokyo, 1987.

Imamura Yoshio. *Shiryō Yagyū Shinkageryū.* Vols. 1–2. Tokyo, 1995.

—. *Yamato Yagyū ichizoku.* Tokyo, 1974.

Imano Nobuo. *Edo no tabi.* Tokyo, 1986.

Ishioka Hisao. *Hyōbōsha no seikatsu.* Tokyo, 1988.

Kaionji Chōgorō. *Bushō retsuden.* Vols. 1–6. Tokyo, 1964.

Kaku Kōzō. *Miyamoto Musashi jiten.* Tokyo, 2001.

Katsube Mitake. *Bushidō*. Tokyo, 1971.

Kawamura Akira. *Miyamoto Musashi*. Tokyo, 1998.

Kitagawa Hiroshi. *Gunkimono no keifu*. Kyoto, 1985.

Kitajima Matsumoto. *Edo jidai*. Tokyo, 1958.

Kojima Hidehiro. *Kengō densetsu*. Tokyo, 1997.

—. *Sugao no kengōtachi*. Tokyo, 1998.

Kuwata Tadachika. *Chosaku-shū*. Vols. 1–10. Tokyo, 1980.

—. *Nihon no kengō*. Vols. 1–5. Tokyo, 1984.

Maki Hidehiko. *Kengō zenshi*. Tokyo, 2003.

Matsumura Hiroshi. *Rekishi monogatari*. Tokyo, 1979.

Maruoka Muneo. *Miyamoto Musashi meihin shūsei*. Tokyo, 1984.

Matsunobu Ichiji. *Miyamoto Musashi zensho*. Tokyo, 2003.

Miki Seiichirō. *Teppo to sono jisai*. Tokyo, 1981.

Mishima Yukio. *Hagakure nyūmon*. Tokyo, 1967.

Mizuno Yasuo. *Sengoku daimyō Asakurashi to Ichijōdani*. Tokyo, 2002.

Muneta Hiroshi. *Miyamoto Musashi*. Tokyo, 1976.

Nagazumi Yasuaki. *Gunki monogatari no sekai*. Tokyo, 1978.

Nakajima Michiko. *Yagyū Sekishūsai Muneyoshi*. Tokyo, 2003.

Nakamura Akira. *Shinkage-ryū Kamiizumi Nobutsuna*. Tokyo, 2004.

Nakamura Kichiji. *Buke no rekishi*. Tokyo, 1967.

Nakanishi Seizō. *Miyamoto Musashi no saigo*. Tokyo, 1987.

—. *Miyamoto Musashi no Shōgai*. Tokyo, 1975.

Nakayama Hakudō. *Kendō kōwa*. Tokyo, 1937.

Nakazato Kaizan. *Nihon bujutsu shinmyō ki*. Tokyo, 1985.

Nanjō Norio. *Nihon no meijō, kojō jiten*. Tokyo, 1999.

Naoki Sukeyama. *Nihon kengō retsuden*. 1983.

Naramoto Tatsuya. *Bushidō no keifu*. Tokyo, 1973.

—. *Gorin no sho nyūmon*. Tokyo, 1984.

Nishigaya Yasuhiro. *Sengoku daimyō jōkaku jiten*. Tokyo, 1999.

Nitobe Inazo. *Bushidō*. Tokyo, 1938.

Okada Kazuo. *Miyamoto Musashi no subete*. Tokyo, 1983.

Okubō Hikozaemon. *Mikawa Monogatari*. Tokyo, 1980.

Ōmori Nobumasa. *Bujutsu densho no kenkyū*. Tokyo, 1991.

Omori Sōgen. *Sho to Zen*. Tkyo, 1973.

—. *Zen no kōsō*. Tokyo, 1979.

Owada Tetsuo. *Sengoku bushō*. Tokyo, 1981.

—. *Toyotomi Hideyoshi*. Tokyo, 1985.

Ozawa Chikamitsu. *Ken shin itchi*. Tokyo, 1978.
Sakai Tadakutsu. *Sekigahara kassen shimatsu ki*. Tokyo, 1991.
Sasamori Junzo. *Ittō-ryū goku-i*. Tokyo, 1986.
Satome Mitsugu. *Jitsuroku Miyamoto Musashi*. Tokyo, 1989.
Shiba Ryōtarō. *Nihon kenkyaku den*. Tokyo, 1982.
—. *Shinsetsu Miyamoto Musashi*. Tokyo, 1983.
So Dōshin. *Shorinji kenpō*. Tokyo, 1963.
Sugimoto Keizaburō. *Gunki monogatari no sekai*. Tokyo, 1985.
Sukeyama Naoki. *Nihon kengō retsuden*. Tokyo, 1983.
Takahashi tomio. *Bushidō no rekishi*. Vols. 1–3. Tokyo, 1986.
Takano Samirō. *Kendō*. Tokyo, 1915.
Takayanagi Kaneyoshi. *Edo no kakyū bushi*. Tokyo, 1980.
Terada Toru. *Dō no shisō*. Tokyo, 1978.
Terayama Tanchū. *Miyamoto Musashi no ken to bi*. Tokyo, 2002.
Tobe Shinichirō. *Kosho Miyamoto Musashi*. Tokyo, 1984.
Tokutomi Sōho. *Kinsei Nihon kokumin-shi*. Tokyo 1982.
Tominaga Kengō. *Shijitsu Miyamoto Musashi*. Tokyo, 1969.
—. *Nihon gassen zenshū*. Vols. 1–6. Tokyo, 1990.
Watatani Kiyoshi. *Nihon kengō no hyakusen*. Tokyo, 1971.
Watanabe Ichirō. *Budō no meichō*. Tokyo, 1979.
Yabushita Hideki. *Miyamoto Musashi densetsu*. Tokyo, 2001.
Yamazaki Masakazu. *Muromachi ki*. Tokyo, 1974.
Yasuda Motohisa. *Bushi sekai no jōmaku*. Tokyo, 1973.
Yasuda Takashi. *Kata no Nihon bunka*. Tokyo, 1984.
Yokoi Kiyoshi. *Chūsei wo ikita hitobito*. Kyoto, 1981.
Yoshida Seiken. *Nitō-ryū o kataru*. Tokyo, 1941.
Yoshida Yutaka. *Budō hiden sho*. Tokyo, 1973.
—. *Zōhyō monogatari*. Tokyo, 1980.

Index

Floating World Editions publishes books that contribute
to a deeper understanding of Asian cultures. Editorial
supervision: Ray Furse. Book and cover design: William
de Lange. Production supervision: Bill Rose. Printing and
binding: Integrated Book Technology. The typefaces used
are Cochin and Cochin Archaic.